Better Homes and Gardens®
Bathroom
Idea File

Meredith® Books
Des Moines, Iowa

Bathroom Idea File
Editor: Paula Marshall
Contributing Editors: Cynthia Pearson, Dan Weeks
Art Director: David Jordan
Copy Chief: Terri Fredrickson
Operations Manager: Karen Schirm
Edit and Design Production Coordinator: Mary Lee Gavin
Managers, Book Production: Pam Kvitne, Marjorie J. Schenkelberg, Rick von Holdt, Mark Weaver
Contributing Copy Editor: Kim Catanzarite
Contributing Proofreaders: Kathi Di Nicola, David Krause, Erin McKay
Contributing Illustrator: Tom Stocki
Indexer: Kathleen Poole
Editorial Assistant: Kaye Chabot

Meredith® Books
Editor in Chief: Linda Raglan Cunningham
Design Director: Matt Strelecki
Managing Editor: Gregory H. Kayko
Executive Editor: Denise L. Caringer

Publisher: James D. Blume
Executive Director, Marketing: Jeffrey Myers
Executive Director, New Business Development: Todd M. Davis
Executive Director, Sales: Ken Zagor
Director, Operations: George A. Susral
Director, Production: Douglas M. Johnston
Business Director: Jim Leonard

Vice President and General Manager: Douglas J. Guendel

Better Homes and Gardens® **Magazine**
Editor in Chief: Karol DeWulf Nickell

Meredith Publishing Group
President, Publishing Group: Stephen M. Lacy
Vice President-Publishing Director: Bob Mate

Meredith Corporation
Chairman and Chief Executive Officer: William T. Kerr

In Memoriam: E. T. Meredith III (1933–2003)

Inspiring Case Studies to Plan Your Bathroom

Welcome to your first step in creating or remodeling your bathroom! Whether you're interested in adding an entire master bath getaway to your home or just want to refresh a dated powder room or dysfunctional family bath, you've come to the right place.

Organized by room type, *Better Homes and Gardens® Bathroom Idea File* is packed with ideas, examples, and solutions. First we talk about the most luxurious and ambitious projects of all: master bath retreats. Whether you're building an entire new wing or carving out space in your current home, we'll give you the lowdown on creating the ultimate in personal pampering spaces.

Of course you don't need to build onto or gut your house to have a luxurious, functional, great-looking bath, and in ensuing chapters, master baths of all sizes, family baths, guest baths, kids' baths, and powder rooms all get their time in the limelight. For each type of bath, we show lots of innovative ideas for making a bath your own.

Then, we get down to brass tacks—or marble vanities—with a comprehensive rundown on the plethora of products and materials that are available to you. These range from familiar and budget-wise to luxurious and exotic. Many are new, and we pay particular attention to those.

Finally our concluding chapter helps you turn your dream bath into a doable project with checklists, project management tips, information on how to select and work with professionals, and a resource section brimming with manufacturers' contact information, websites, organizations, publications, and other sources of invaluable information.

Have a look! Browse this book as you would a gallery of baths or a home tour featuring the most innovative architecture and design—but one that lets you skip the rest of the house and walk directly into the room that will most help you with your next project: the bathroom. Jot down ideas, dog-ear the pages, fill out the worksheets, use the room design kit. Your new bathroom awaits you!

Everyone needs a quiet, peaceful area in the home in which to get away from it all. For most, that place is the bathroom. Long revered as a fully legitimate place to hide, the bathroom shuns the incessantly ringing phone and eludes the demands of hectic daily life. It's no surprise that master baths—adjacent to yet another legitimate retreat, the bedroom—have expanded to soothe and revive with cushy reading lounges, minikitchens, fitness nooks, and private balconies. These spaces masquerade as parts of the bathroom, so users feel sheltered, safe, and unavailable when they use them.

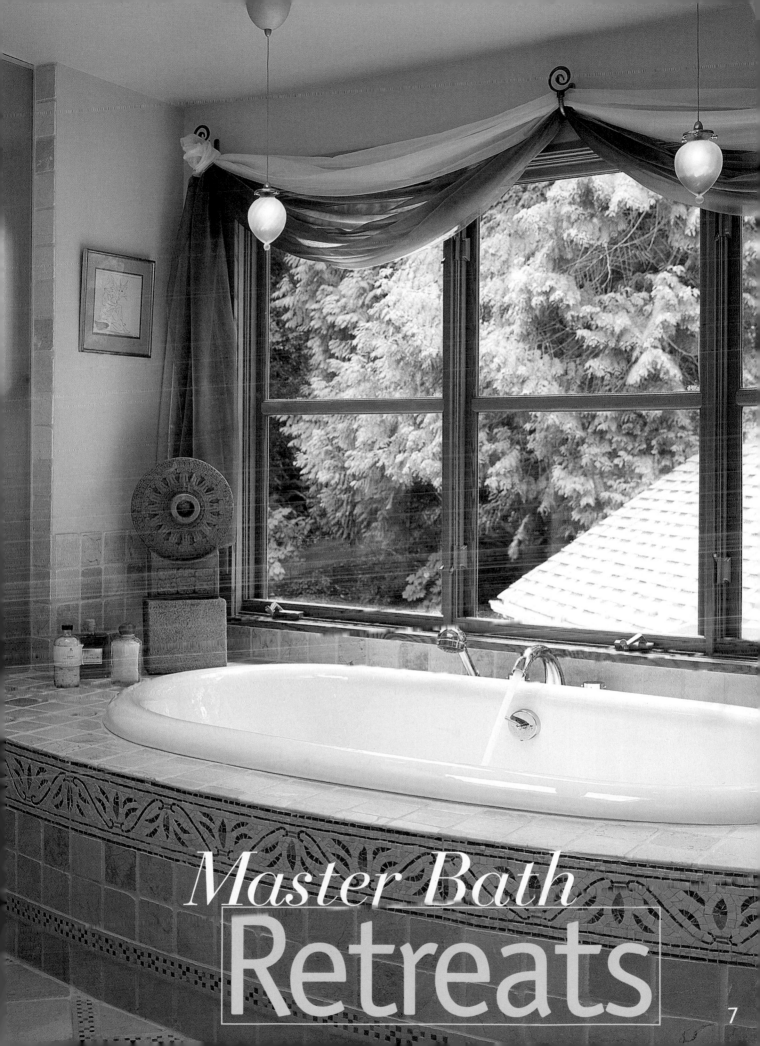

Master Bath Retreats

A New Suite Takes Wing

BEDROOM

BATH

CLOSET

Ground-floor addition

Even grand old homes sometimes have master bedrooms that are pretty basic. Here a back wing yields luxury while preserving the farmhouse look.

An addition off an existing covered porch was the route to a master suite getaway with this house built in 1844. The look is in keeping with many of the Northeast's older houses, which feature a succession of rooms tacked on over the years. A dressing, toilet, and bathing area occupy the half of the addition closest to the street. The back portion is a sunroomlike bedroom with a sitting area that opens onto a backyard patio and covered porch. Grass-green wall paint echoes the outdoor hues. The floor features salvaged chestnut boards that once lined an attic. A large upholstered chair and ottoman create a bedside reading area; a table nook in the corner nearest the porch serves breakfast, newspaper reading, and

1

personal computer pursuits. Two windows light up the front-facing half of the suite, which includes a bathing space and an all-glass shower stall. The dressing space also has a window. A private toilet area and a closet-enclosed minikitchen are neatly wedged in between.

Dressing Room

Wide-plank chestnut floors, a richly colored rug, and a broad bench create a warm setting in this white-painted closet/dressing room. A west-facing window brightens the space and provides daylight for dressing. The bench is handy when pulling on socks and shoes and also for laying out a suitcase and packing right in the closet—a much simpler solution than carrying clothes in and out to a suitcase on the bed.

Measuring 12×11 feet, this room actually is three closets: one for each homeowner and a utility closet that's tucked behind the door. The shoe racks imitate a shoe store design—there are two here, on opposite walls—and they're useful for belts, hats, and purses as well. Walls are fitted with peg holes for shelf-mounting flexibility.

1 *Architectural themes from the main house and porch carry across the hallway to the suite, where window shape, positioning, and arches parallel those of the house and porch.*

2 *Slate floor tiles in earthy hues ground the light-as-air white bathing space. An easy-to-reach towel rack hovers over the European-style tub.*

3 *A coffee bar nestles next to the linen closet. The under-counter refrigerator is handy for stocking beverages.*

1 *A table, chairs, and an Internet connection on a nearby wall make a private place for sharing a bit of breakfast, reading the paper, or writing e-mail away from household hubbub.*

2 *Room from the adjoining porch made possible a glass-walled hallway leading from the main house to the master suite. The porch retains its open feel thanks to the hall's floor-to-ceiling windows.*

3 *The suite's windows are fitted with white draperies for those rare occasions when muted daylight is preferred.*

Home Away from Home

Freestanding master suite

Sometimes the best way to add on is to add—but not on. This freestanding master suite, separate from the main house, allows the owners a spacious private retreat.

1

Detaching this suite from the original structure had many advantages: Construction didn't disrupt the existing house, the suite was sited to take best advantage of the spectacular ocean views, and finally, its placement created a patio with a hot tub and eating area between the buildings—great for outdoor living and entertaining.

Located within the walls of a Japanese-inspired pavilion, the master suite mimics the post-and-beam construction of the main house. In addition to unifying the old and new spaces, this architecture creates an unconfining, free feeling, which is enhanced by windows that stretch from ceiling nearly to the floor. The suite feels much larger than its 675 square feet. The post-and-beam design also provides a way to work around the topographic challenges of the site—the vertical posts driven into the rocky hillside support a floor plan that projects out over the slope. As a result the new pavilion seems to float above the exposed granite outcropping.

Angling away from the rest of the house, the master suite captures the best of the ocean sights without intruding on the light and views in existing rooms. A new terrace area
continued

1 *The master bath, like the bedroom, capitalizes on seaside views. The shower floor features small pieces of polished slate; the tub surround is granite.*

2 *A curved black granite counter adds drama to the double vanity and complements the gray and tan slate bathroom floor.*

3 *Minimal furnishings and large windows encourage bay views to dominate the room. The maple bed and night tables, which are built into one of the closet walls, complement the clean look of the suite's post-and-beam construction.*

4 *The central closet limits clutter thanks to full-length wardrobes and drawers for socks and sweaters. A mirror at one end reflects a painting hanging in the passageway.*

also connects the old and new spaces and provides outdoor living space that's accessible from both the new suite and the main living room.

The suite's interior follows a minimalist design that maximizes the limited space. The two passageways around a central closet lead to the bathroom at the back. This layout successfully divides the large room into bedroom and bath while retaining an open feeling. One closet wall serves as the bed's headboard; the opposite wall doubles as the backboard for the vanity. Both provide added benefit: walls for artwork that don't impede the spectacular view.

1 An etched-glass screen ensures privacy for the shower. The sandblasted design is an abstract representation of the home's post-and-beam structure.

2 Maple cabinetry surrounds the gas fireplace and hides the TV and stereo equipment when they're not in use. The built-ins also provide display space for artwork.

3 The master suite pavilion appears almost to float above the hillside. Slate steps lead down to the new bluestone terrace, which features a spa and dining area.

1

2

An Everyday Vacation

Touches of Tuscany

With its rich materials, sensual pleasures, romantic lighting, and a great view, this European-style bath is a feast for the senses.

From the high-backed soaking tub surrounded by candles to the dimable lighting and soft music, this master bath provides everything you need for an everyday vacation. Marble, faux weathered ceramic tile, and distressed cabinetry mix to create a welcoming retreat reminiscent of Tuscany. Columns flank the whirlpool tub, objets d'art grace recessed nooks, and Victorian-style faucets contribute to the European theme.

In fact the room appeals to all of the senses. Radiant heat flooring, satin-nickel fixtures, and handmade felt rugs offer tactile delight. The steam shower relaxes tired muscles. A view of a pond through the window draws the eye, while built-in
continued

1 The total effect is the result of well-coordinated details: The unique marble chair rail and border complement ceramic wall tile and elegant marble countertops.
2 Luxury reigns in this lavish, 12×17-foot bath with an attached 6×15-foot sunroom/breakfast nook. Rich-looking marble, weathered tile, and felt rugs grace the retreat.
3 French doors lead from the master bathroom to a sunroom that offers a quiet spot to enjoy breakfast or an evening beverage without leaving the suite.

Breakfast in Bed

Microwave ovens and refrigerators have yet to become standard master suite features, but it may be only a matter of time before they do. Designers report a growing demand for suites that include spaces where the homeowners can enjoy morning coffee or evening drinks.

What started as a luxury is now thought of as a convenience. Houses are becoming larger. In addition it is easier to have a kitchenette in the master suite than it is to walk through 2,000 square feet of house just to get to the toaster.

The most elaborate setups are fully equipped minikitchens that may include wine racks, wet bars, and dining areas. The cabinetry, countertops, appliances, and other components of such spaces can easily run $10,000.

If you have a more modest house, you can still enjoy some of the conveniences: Build a space for a cappuccino maker into the cabinetry or, even easier, set up a coffeemaker on the vanity.

2

speakers, wired to a central home stereo system, fill the space with soothing music.

Even the sense of taste benefits in this bath, which features its own dining area. A set of French doors leads to a new sunroom that includes a minikitchen, cafe table, and comfy chair, allowing the homeowners to fix a quick breakfast or enjoy an evening glass of wine without having to leave the suite. Three walls of windows draw light into the sunroom and bathroom beyond. The bathroom also connects to a dressing room with built-in cherry cabinets, plenty of space for hanging clothes, and a center island.

1 The sunroom features the same level of quality and detailing as does the bath. A bar sink, paneled refrigerator, coffeemaker, and wine rack—in addition to a swivel-mounted, flat-screen TV—ensure that breakfast, snacks, beverages, and entertainment are close at hand.
2 Marble columns—a prime platform for candlesticks—flank the soaking tub. Combined with fully dimable lighting, the candlelight adds to the romantic ambiance of the bath.

1

Open to View

Top-floor contemporary suite

The advantages to building "up" include privacy, lots of window light, and sweeping views.

If you're lucky enough to have the option of locating a master suite on the top floor, you may be able to create a free-flowing bed/bath combination similar to this one. The tub, raised on a tiled platform above three bench-size steps, is the focal point of the room: a clean-lined, contemporary space that invites the outdoors in.

There are no walls to divide bedroom from bath although one space is for sleeping and the other provides for grooming and bathing. In lieu of furnishings, light-stained, clean-lined wood cabinetry store clothes and personal items. The blond built-ins blend with the yellow-green walls and carpet, making the space feel larger and eliminating the need for an intrusive, walled-off closet.

Facing the bed in mid-room, a TV hangs industrial-style. Behind *continued*

1 *The back of the vanity area serves as a minimalist room divider, with a wood panel that matches other cabinetry in the bedroom area. The TV is suspended from the ceiling for comfy viewing.*

2 *The tub may well be the best seat in this hilltop house. Steps covered with 1-inch tile squares lead the way to the strategically placed soaking spot and also provide storage and seating. A picture window offers panoramic views.*

3 *The shower stall fits between the tub and vanities; its glass walls allow views of nature. The lower portions of the walls are sandblasted for partial privacy.*

4 *A counterweighted patio window glides down in its tracks, opening the bath area to an upper-level patio. When the window is open, bathers feel like they're in an outdoor hot tub.*

1 *Dual vanities free-float beside an island of tile. The exposed sinks are flanked by shelves and are separated by drawers built into a center column.*
2 *To maximize space and minimize clutter, the suite has no closets. Instead built-in storage units with pocket doors flank the bed.*
3 *Sleek drawers and kitchenlike upper cabinets unobtrusively hug the room's walls.*
4 *Angled walls, clever built-ins, and a partitionless design result in a comfortable, contemporary sleeping-bath area.*

the TV a wood panel and a column of tile rise from a tile platform and partially divide the sleeping and bathing areas. On the bath side of the wood partition, twin sinks flank a tiled cabinet with four drawers. The shower fits in neatly beside the steps to the tub. Clear glass shower walls provide a spectacular 360-degree view.

With its dark blue tile, the raised bath is like an island amid a sea of greenish yellow. It's a color scheme that softens the primary hues—yellow, blue, and the occasional red—into comfortable variations. Natural light enhances the palette. Window walls on three sides of the room offer views at every turn. A triangular bench built into one window wall is a great spot for quiet contemplation.

To avoid boxiness the window walls angle outward and the varied ceiling height pitches at an angle in some places. The ceiling shoots upward over the tub, for example, to create a sense of spaciousness.

Although the suite seems open to the world, privacy is not a problem—a hilltop lot and upper-story placement means those outside the house can't see in.

2
3

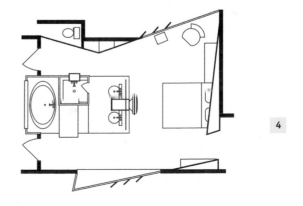

1

Manor-House
Magic

Remodeling a vintage space
This lush and spacious master suite was once a tangle of tiny bedrooms, baths, and closets.

Even more remarkable than its cramped beginnings is this suite's lavish French-English manor-house look. This renovation is proof that a clean-slate approach can result in a coveted old-time architecture—in this case from 1936. It's all in the details: dark-stained millwork, old-growth oak flooring, textured tile, chandeliers and antiques, and layers of wallpaper, draperies, and upholstery. In recomposing the spaces, care was taken to create a sense of entry to each area by moving from small, low-ceilinged spaces, such as the paneled arches, to larger, more open rooms. Paneled arches take care of the low aspects while a tray ceiling, such as the one in the bedroom, achieves a sense of height. The tray ceiling also gives an otherwise boxy room a grown-up, shapely quality. It was achieved by blowing out the existing eight-foot ceiling and taking the tray, which rises and narrows over the room, into the attic.

1 An array of tumbled and textured tiles give the bath lush character. Mossy green draperies, deep green vine wallpaper, and soft sconce lighting warm the space. The location of the tub faucet—center of the near side—allows a couple to comfortably face one another and soak.

2 Built of three custom cabinetry pieces—sink, storage, dressing table—the vanity looks like a richly detailed piece of furniture.

3 A glass surround visually minimizes the large presence of the shower in a galley bath space. Textured tile within adds antiquity.

4 Similar to ventilated transom windows over a door, hopper windows in the shower aid airflow and break the modern look of tall glass panels.

5 The high ceilings in the bathroom are offset with tile that climbs the wall and outlines the top of the door. A band of relief tile adds textures and a finishing detail.

1 The tray ceiling in the bedroom adds another dimension to the space while framing a Scottish-style thistle-and-glass chandelier.

2 The round sink in the wet bar is fashioned of hammered satin nickel.

3 An antique oak fireplace surround and old-growth oak floors combine with rich, deep colors and vintage furnishings to give the sitting room warm character.

4 Inserts of old glass dressed with hand-painted acanthus leaves decorate the upper cabinets of the wet bar.

5 The homeowners renovated the original two bedrooms, the sitting room between them, plus a tiny bath and closets to make room for a luxurious bath, a wet bar, and dressing room.

3
4

BEFORE

AFTER

5

Big, Bold &
Natural

Day-lit master suite

Huge windows and strategically placed
skylights allow the natural materials in
this open suite to glow and sparkle.

Awoodland sanctuary is one
of this master's amenities,
thanks to huge window walls that
make the most of their presence. The
deck and rail balcony
just outside is unobtrusive—not
distracting from the view.
The geometrically shaped bed frame,
bench, chair and matching ottoman,
and chaise fill out the huge room
in a variety of shapes and colors.
Plush fabrics including silk, wool,
and chenille soften the large pieces.
On the walls, tawny custom
wallpaper, which is applied in
randomly torn pieces, offers both
subtle color and texture.

1 *Velvety expanses of rustic slate tiles
warm this light-filled space. Maple laminate
cabinets provide color and storage. Free-
form drawer pulls sparkle against the solid
background.*

The sky-lit, spalike ambience of
the adjacent bath recalls the colors
and textures of the outdoors. Huge
mirrors echo the bedroom's windows
and reflect the bath's soothing yellow
walls, expanses of stone countertop,
earthy slate tiles, and smooth maple
cabinets. Free-form faucet handles
and cabinetry pulls give a quirky
naturalism. A terrycloth shower
curtain is in keeping with spa style.

Play the Angles

Contemporary style sometimes spurns the relentlessly rectilinear rules and throws in a
curve. This suite, for instance, features plenty of the sharp-edged geometry for which
contemporary architecture is known. The boxy shape of the rooms is reinforced by big
rectangular windows, skylights, mirrors, storage cubes, and the cube-form vanity stool.
In this bath, however, a gracefully curved vanity top and dressing table area offer a
welcome counterpoint, softening the rooms' lines. The tendril-like handles on the
faucets and drawers follow their lead. In the adjoining bedroom, the headboard and the
upholstered furniture echo the theme.

1

2

3

1 *Sunlight fills the bathing area through a skylight overhead. Slate tiles need no accents or detailing; they're a visual feast all by themselves. Set in a surround of stone tiles, the bright white, soaking tub looks fresh and crisp as do the terrycloth towels and shower curtain*

2 *Twining faucet handles are both contemporary and organic.*

3 *Clean lines, gentle curves, and geometric shapes characterize this master bedroom/sitting area. The bold shapes of the furnishings complement the scale of woodland view.*

Redwood Redux

What if you need more space, but your house is a classic that you're reluctant to disturb? That was the case with this house, designed in the 1950s by a protégé of Frank Lloyd Wright. It combines beautiful materials—most notably the redwood paneling and woodwork throughout—and clean, intriguing details. Designed for a couple, the house originally had only two bedrooms, a full bath, and a half bath. Family life dictated the addition of a master suite, but the original floor plan was so effective, coupled with charming detailing throughout, that it seemed a shame to disturb it with a remodeling job.

The solution was a two-story addition that has a design and uses materials that respect the original. Most of the new space is included in an upstairs master suite with a bedroom, bath, small exercise room, and terrace. Downstairs the addition comprised a sunroom and bath. Prolific use of redwood and careful attention to craftsmanship and detailing combine to create rooms that look original to the house.

The bed is recessed into a three-foot window bay, which was designed so that the bedroom retained the proportions of the rooms in the original home while accommodating a large bed without crowding. Redwood is used for

woodwork and trim throughout. A soffit above the bed conceals the ductwork and vents for the heating and cooling system. In the bath similar detailing conceals lights and a speaker system.

As in the original home, natural materials are emphasized: The bathroom countertops are limestone, and the bedroom walls are papered with rice paper. The result is a classic home that has grown to meet the needs of a growing family.

3
4

5

1 The frosted glass panel and circular mirror capture the light streaming in through two tall windows on the opposite wall. Towers on either side of the vanity replace a typical linen closet.

2 Crafted of aluminum, mahogany, and beech, the custom cabinetry and straightforward hardware echo the home's linear design.

3 Windows embrace the master bath's whirlpool bath, wrapping seamlessly around the corner. Lights and speakers—concealed in the redwood unit above the tub—add an interesting architectural touch.

4 Handmade tiles, a faucet and spout integrated with the backsplash, and a vibrant above-counter sink introduce just enough color.

5 The two-story addition includes a sunroom and extra bath on the main floor and a master suite on the upper. The architecture of the addition—true to the original house—suggests it has always been there.

1 1

2

1 *A concrete tower supports the bath's second sink. It is the center of a symmetrical composition created with mahogany cabinets and two tall windows flanking a mirror. The concrete intentionally matches the tones and texture of the limestone cabinet tops.*

2 *Rice paper wallcoverings, redwood detailing, and a custom-made mahogany bed and bedside table complement the original architecture of this classic Frank Lloyd Wright-style home.*

3 *Redwood paneling lines the walls surrounding the bedroom's cozy built-in window seat. Doors on either side of the seat open to two ample storage closets.*

3

Modern Day
Mediterranean

Expanding the top half-story

If your house is a story and a half, you probably have more room to expand than you think.

Positioned over a full level, this half-story master bedroom and bath in a 1920s Spanish Mediterranean home yielded an easy expansion. Adding a cantilevered bump-out to the bathroom and stretching the half story to meet the perimeter of the level below made room for a luxurious suite. The expansion draws on the old-world Mediterranean architectural style and decorative themes from other parts of the home, incorporating up-to-date entertainment and personal care features. A combination of cream, honey, and black—rendered in the lush furnishings and materials—makes up a rich and refreshing color scheme.

1 The old-world style suits the owners' aesthetic tastes and the 1920s Spanish Mediterranean architecture of the home. At the suite's vanity wall, two broad-rimmed sinks are supported by a hutch cabinet and shelves in wall niches on either side. A wrought-iron chandelier draws the eye to the vaulted ceiling, emphasizing spaciousness and grandeur.

2 A small television snugs into a tub-area niche to serve the bath. For safety a bolt holds the TV in place and wiring runs into the master bedroom.

3 The suite's tub area takes advantage of the 30-inch cantilevered bump-out that was added during the remodeling. Fresh towels and bathing supplies are stored in a glass-shelved niche that echoes those near the vanities. The tub's tiled arch as well as the mirrors and shower stall help soften the room with their curved edges.

4 The luxuries in this gateway include a sauna and adjacent steam shower. The bench, rainfall-style showerhead, and flexible handheld shower afford many bathing options.

37

1

2

1 *The floor of the dressing area is two steps up from the bedroom. Its vanity and closet door design match those found elsewhere in the home. An island offers a surprisingly useful surface; shoes and suitcases store underneath.*

2 *The smartly built island includes a pullout tray and shallow drawer for small grooming items.*

3 *Pushing the perimeter of an existing master bed-and-bath made room for a luxurious upper level getaway. A cantilevered bump-out supports the tub area, the bathroom crept into the bedroom space, and the new bedroom now extends over the existing main level.*

4 *Pushing the master bedroom out 10 feet (the overhead beam marks the wall's original location) made room for a sitting area and fireplace modeled after the old one. A new, traditionally styled armoire houses an entertainment system and mini fridge.*

5 *The fridge keeps late-night snacks and morning fare close at hand.*

3

MASTER BEDROOM
15x18

BATH

W D

BEFORE

MASTER BEDROOM
15x22

DN

DRESSING
14x16

BATH
11x17

ATTIC

W D

CLOS

AFTER

From Fifties to
Fabulous

Expanding a ranch
One-story ranch houses generate terrific remodeling potential.

At their best, 1950s ranch houses offer generous square footage arranged in convenient, one-level plans that are particularly appealing to today's busy lifestyles. Their outmoded interior design, however, is not generally coveted. A lot of pink tiles and shag carpets have survived the years. Bedrooms, even those of good size, often lack enough natural light to suit most people's needs. Fortunately these single-story houses are generally easy to open up. Big windows, patios, and other outdoor living areas are only a saw cut away.

The master suite in this home is an example of what can happen when the determination to add more light and space takes hold. A modest 8×15-foot addition is completely glass-walled, visually expanding into the great outdoors. At the same time, *continued*

1

1 Natural elements set the tone for an indoor/outdoor bath. Tennessee Crab Orchard stone, used outside for the shower walls, continues indoors, separated only by the glass wall.
2 Plantings of bamboo and a crushed granite floor contribute to the natural feel of the shower.
3 Outside the addition a sandstone patio framed with a limestone wall offers a place for quiet contemplation. The paint color on the conservatory structure was chosen to blend with the environment.
4 The courtyard serves as an enclosed play area for the homeowner's children.

builders completely reconfigured the inside of the room. A wall of closets with Baltic birch doors replace the original mazelike entry. The wall also minimizes the need for new furniture. Two nightstands and an easy chair for reading are all that is needed to complete the room.

The adjoining bath was similarly transformed. Once a brown tile room half its current size, the bath was transformed into a light-filled space. The new configuration borrows space from a walk-in closet that was made redundant by the bedroom built-ins. The Baltic birch cabinetry is repeated in this room, creating continuity from the bedroom. An added feature is a window wall—complete with a door that opens to an outdoor shower. Inside modern lines and materials create a clean—yet warm—environment. The tub surround, floor, and partition wall are all constructed of finished concrete. Radiant heat elements in the floor warm all three to the touch on chilly mornings. Reeded glass tops the partition between the vanity and the toilet, providing privacy while admitting diffused, filtered light to the room.

1 An 8×15 conservatory bump-out brings the outdoors in with a cypress-framed window wall.
2 The built-in closets end short of the window wall, creating a shelved nook for display opportunities.
3 Light and simplicity characterize this remodeled bedroom. The original clerestory windows provide privacy; a glass-top wall behind the bed admits light from the adjoining bath's skylight. Baltic birch built-in closets and refinished oak floors keep the space spare and uncluttered, yet warm.

2

3

For those who want a luxurious bathroom with plenty of elbowroom—but none of the mini apartment amenities, a master bath suite is the answer. Long on space and deep in personal pampering options, these suites forgo library nooks and snack bars, devoting their square footage to traditional master suite activities: sleeping, bathing, and grooming. What these suites give up in versatility—compared to the master retreats featured in Chapter One—they make up for in spaciousness, simplicity, and ease of design. The options for achieving them are endless. You'll get ideas here!

Master Bath
Suites

Curtain Call
Creativity

The plan for this bath is smart, but its magic lies in its materials and execution. Humble or plain elements share space with unexpected ones.

Call it innovative, call it clever, call it beautiful. This galley bath features three compartments along the back wall—tub, toilet, and shower—which the users can instantly hide with a sweep of two Copper-colored silk curtain panels. The goal was to create an unbounded master bath of modern,

elegant, "unbathroomy" appeal.

The plan is simple. A 19½×8½ rectangle is separated from the bedroom via a "floating wall." Three compartments line the back wall and the floating wall supports two pedestal sinks. The arrangement is plenty roomy for two—no traffic jams here.

The painted brick exterior wall hints at the original commercial nature of the loft home. A basic white tub is wrapped in exotic Philippine mahogany; hardwood covers the floors; and dramatic

BATH
19½×8½

MASTER BEDROOM

copper silk curtains conceal any or all of the back wall compartments. All very "unbathroomy" materials indeed. Meanwhile the tone-on-tone color scheme sizzles like spices in a saute pan: curry walls, copper silk, rich mahogany, honey hardwood, taupe brick, and milky-white sinks. It's a look that's, earthy, elegant, and ultimately, fresh.

1

2 3
4

1 The shower is a simple box of intriguing honey-hued limestone tiles with an inset ledge for supplies. When the water is on, a nylon liner pulls out from behind the curtain.

2 Recessing the fixed mirror panels over the sinks and 2 inches into the wall produces a window-like look. Toiletries stash on wheeled steel carts that can roll from sink to shower as needed.

3 The rich grain of a mahogany surround warms the chill of a white porcelain tub. Taupe-painted brick walls play harmony to copper-colored silk curtain panels.

4 Silk curtains conceal the tub, toilet, and shower compartments on demand.

5 The handheld showerhead is handy for rinsing. The mahogany tub surround is finished with a waterproof tub sealer.

5
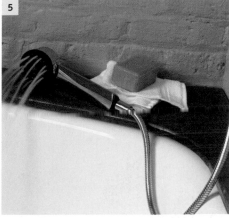

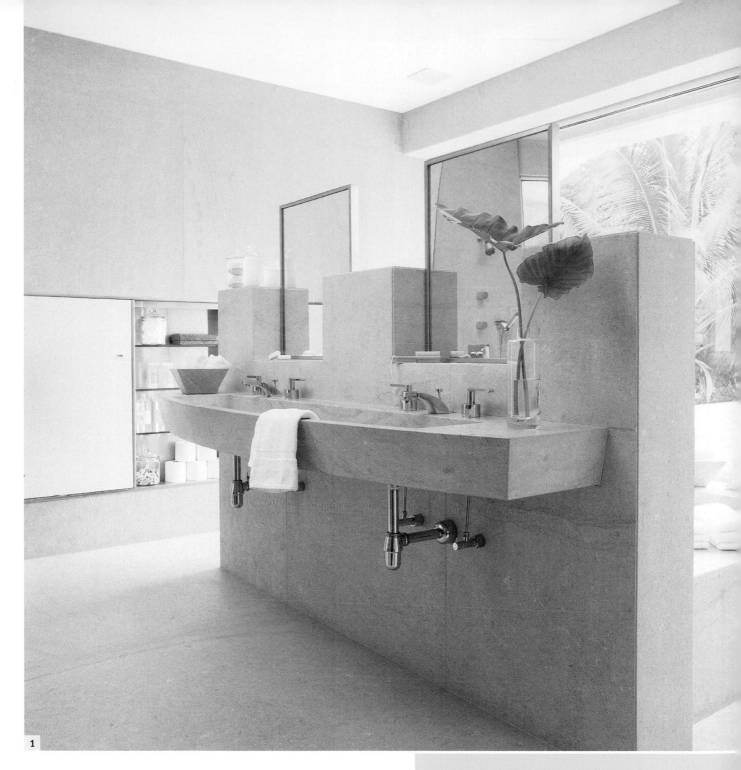

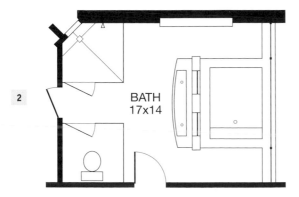

BATH
17x14

1 A trough-style sink for two is visually calmer than two separate sinks. Two prep stations fitted with faucets, mirrors, and a deep ledge for toiletries provide plenty of room for side-by-side grooming.

2 The bath feels bright and open thanks to frosted glass toilet and shower enclosures. The tub steps are positioned for a picture window view.

3 A long vertical window in the shower allows a view of the courtyard garden but is high enough off the ground for privacy. A similar glass enclosure surrounds the toilet across the room.

4 The toiletries niche includes a mirror wedge, ideal for shaving in the shower.

Zen and the Art of Stone

A contemporary bath is rock solid

"Stone" traditionally connotes a cool look, but this isn't marble here—it's limestone and the look is warm.

Limestone is an increasingly popular choice for baths, and it's easy to see why. Compared with granite and marble, it inspires a completely different response. Limestone looks warm, it feels good to the touch, and its subtle graining imparts a woodlike intrigue. In this large, luxurious bath, limestone covers nearly every surface. The bath includes very few elements: blond limestone joins glass, simple fixtures, stainless-steel-framed mirrors, and a medicine cabinet with frosted glass doors. The look is both clean and inviting; it's a calm-inspiring oasis away from everyday chaos.

1 *The half-wall of the vanity, punctuated with stainless framed mirrors, separates the soaking tub area from the rest of the bath without blocking light or views.*

2 *Behind the vanity is a dramatic, step-down soaking tub. The fixtures appear to be a pair of faucets, but actually are a faucet and handheld shower.*

3 *Stainless-steel and frosted glass medicine cabinets feature interior lights that cast a gentle glow. The cabinets fit snugly into an exterior wall and are positioned for easy access from the shower, tub, and vanities.*

About Limestone

Limestone is becoming a popular choice for baths even though it's softer and more permeable than granite. Here's why:

- It's durable and easy to maintain when properly sealed.
- Slabs of limestone combine in a near-seamless application, minimizing grout lines.
- Manufacturers carve limestone slabs into sinks and tubs, niches, ledges, and benches.
- Limestone is available in a range of hues, and its subtle grain adds texture to monochromatic settings.
- Manufacturers bevel, hone, or polish limestone for finished looks that combine easily.
- Cool to the touch, limestone is visually warm.
- Limestone is plentiful and has stood the test of time.

2

3

The Great Indoors

A family-size jetted tub basks in a window-wrapped niche for year-round relaxation. It's an ideal substitute for a hot tub in less-than-ideal climates.

Outdoor hot tubs are great, but if you live in a cold climate, they pose some disadvantages. Not everyone likes the contrast between frozen hair and a tropical trunk—not to mention painfully cold trips in and out of the steamy water. Then there's the cost of keeping the water hot, day in and day out. This bath bypasses these hassles by bringing the spa inside. A family-size jetted tub is the focal point, set in aqua-colored tiles in its own niche, with casement windows that open wide to admit mild-season breezes.

continued

1 Tall mirrors, clear basins, and a curved-edge top that resembles a living room coffee table set this vanity apart from the ordinary. Glass tiles and gleaming fittings add to the reflective theme.

2 A frosted glass door and window bring light into the toilet room without sacrificing privacy. The room's brightness adds to the spalike feeling.

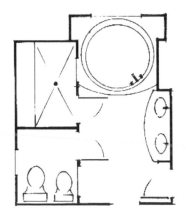

With year-round views of the home's deck and backyard, it's one step away from being outdoors. A steam/shower room adjacent to the tub features a 6-foot-long bench for sitting or reclining. A glass door, a window, and a glass ceiling with skylights flood the compartment with light. A toilet and bidet share a private alcove that's also topped with a skylight. Elsewhere the room sparkles with spun-glass lavatory bowls, a plate-glass vanity, and a pair of large mirrors. Wall-mounted faucets projecting through mirrors seem to magically hover above the sculpted glass sink bowls. Shelf niches in the wall opposite the vanity hold linens and lotions.

2

3

1 The blue and green glass-tile tub motif continues from the main bath area into the spacious steam-shower room. The tiles' blue squares suggest a chair rail, with a nod to the home's Victorian-era detailing.

2 The soothing, water-like hues around the tub also relate to the trees and plantings in the yard. Opening the windows brings breezes inside, adding to the fresh-air ambiance. Built-in shelves hold linens.

3 A second set of showerheads and controls at the other end of the shower room makes it possible for two to clean up simultaneously. Sunflower-size shower heads provide a thorough soaking.

1

On the Angle

In a modern home where no room is square, this master bath fits right in. Its angled approach could work equally well in more conventional homes.

This bath manages to both flaunt convention and practice good design. In fact its large space might seem limiting if divided into a maze of cubicles. Here the vanity, whirlpool tub, and shower are placed on the diagonal and separated with partial walls no more than 6 feet, 3 inches tall. The spaces angle toward the room's sole window; a skylight above draws even more light into the room. Neutral colors and natural materials soften the angles and clean-lined architecture of the bath. The pink and gray tones of the polished marble vanity are sleek but earthy. Honey-color cabinetry with a highly textured grain takes the formal edge off the marble. Fixtures are traditional in style. The result is a pleasing tension between modern and traditional, upscale and ordinary, that ultimately succeeds in creating an ambience that's warm, inviting, and practical too.

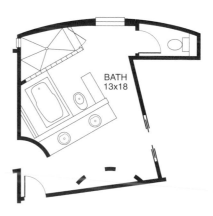

BATH
13x18

Well Angled

Dividing a 13×18-foot room without creating cramped spaces requires features that boost spaciousness.

• Interior walls are angled toward the room's single window to take advantage of daylight.

• A glass block wall and frameless glass door let light shine through and make the shower feel bigger.

• Partial partitions allow light and views to fill the room, and create a flowing floor plan.

• A subdued color palette—white walls, pink-tone marble, honey-hued wood—soften the room's angles.

1 Stepping back from the tub, slim marble shelves climb the wall in ziggurat style. The shelves' design finesses the tricky junction between the diagonal-placed vanity meets right-angled walls.

2 The room's unusual splayed walls create an area that's both spacious and intimate.

3 The vanity wall offers open shelving for towel storage and creates privacy around the tub without a full enclosure. The glass block beyond is a shower wall.

Suite Calm

A few carefully chosen furnishings and minimal color evoke soothing elegance in this bath suite.

When daily life fills you with discord, sensory underload may be just what you need to feel refreshed and revived. That was the goal in this bath suite, where lots of space is devoted to limited—though important—function for a luxurious, undecorated feel.

Obtaining the space was easy. A bedroom and adjacent sun porch in an older home were converted to the main bath and soaking tub, respectively. A well-edited blend of color and texture creates the soothing atmosphere. Creamy painted walls and an abundance of window light plus limestone floor tiles warm the pristine milky-white fixtures and trim paint. A tubside laminate caddy and a nutty-brown velvet chair echo the vanity and dresser's textured caramel-to-espresso tones. Brushed stainless-steel fixtures and an oversize, silver-frame mirror add a sleek, contemporary edge. The minimalist approach is calming, but with its texture and tension, it also has the power to revive.

1 *A bedroom and sun porch in a turn-of-the-century home become a sleek, elegant bath suite. Light from the many windows bathes the spaces.*

2 *Leaning casually against the wall, a huge silver mirror reflects light and serves grooming needs. A brown velvet chair nearby is handy for sitting to pull on shoes.*

3 *The vanity island serves the toilet and shower, and it's not too far from the bath porch. The narrow dresser's deep-espresso stain contrasts the vanity table's warmer tone. Limestone floors have a caramel shade that bridges the suite's cream-to-cocoa hues.*

4 *Two white Philippe Starck vessel sinks are mounted and plumbed on an antique table. You see the minimalist ingredient scheme here: glossy porcelain, brushed stainless, and rough-textured warm wood.*

5 *Ladder-style shelves keep supplies within reach of the tub and carry wood tones to the bath porch.*

1 *Adjacent to the bath suite a walk-in closet's custom racks, shelves, and drawers organize belts, ties, shoes, and clothing.*
2 *A faucet and jewelry-like drain chain adorn the chunky, curvaceous tub.*
3 *Small tiles laid herringbone-style on the bathing porch have so much texture they look similar to a sisal rug.*
4 *Glossy, milk-white tiles in a railroad pattern rise two-thirds the height of the walls. Molding and detail tiles finish the top edge; a plain metal knob holds a towel.*
5 *Devoted solely to bathing, this room's space and window views are the luxuries here. A black laminate caddy pulls up close to hold a glass of wine; the tub faucet's centered position allows a bather to recline in either direction.*

4

5

In the Buff

The peachy hue of natural travertine stars in this less-is-luxe bath suite.

Natural, unpolished travertine marble has an organic, rosy-flesh color to it that casts a flattering glow through this master bath. The stone's naturally occurring crevices and pits are coated with clear, non-yellowing sealer to yield a smooth surface that has a rough and raw appearance. Here it's used in near seamless stretches for countertop, bath area floor, tub, and shower. Lines in this bath are clean but all—from the bullnose countertop edge to the cabinetry trim, steel door pulls, and arch between vanity and bathing area—are based on circles. The curves add a pleasing softness that, creates a comfortable place to undress.

With its vaulted ceilings and walls that reach for the roof, the bath feels much larger than it actually is. The mirrored wall of the vanity rises to the peak, encasing a narrow window between the sinks. A roller blind pulls down for privacy when needed. The bathing area's window features graduated sandblasting for complete bathing privacy without blocked light or views. The choice of a combination tub-shower won over separate units; luxurious materials and features that serve both purposes fill the bill. A nearly invisible barrier of clear glass encloses the tub to the ceiling, sealing the shower for steam. A small toilet room is tucked behind the tub, while a door offers full privacy.

1

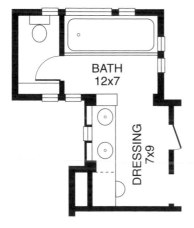

BATH
12x7

DRESSING
7x9

1 Recessed medicine chests are part of this mirrored wall configuration, which rises to the ceiling. Wrought-iron sconces with art glass shades are sculpture in their own right. Dark-stained wood floors in the vanity area ground the light colors.

2 The use of limited materials creates a lush, expansive feel in the tub area: travertine marble for the tub, floor, and walls; a frameless glass shower with two heads; and a minimally trimmed window gradually sandblasted to offer privacy, light, and views.

3 High-end standard tubs with price tags as high as custom work helped the homeowners choose this custom tub. It's carved from travertine slabs, angled for comfort, and scored on the bottom for slip resistance.

4 A dressing table space in the vanity area offers a comfy spot grooming place.

1

Antique Meets
Modern

1 A local artisan remade the antique dresser as a marble-topped vanity. An under-the-floor heating system is an inconspicuous modern touch that boosts comfort.

2 Transposing the bathroom and dressing room improved traffic flow and privacy in this addition.

3 An antique dressing table, mirror, and stool are snugged into a niche between the shower and the toilet areas.

Rearranging an old home's tacked-on addition creates a graceful master bath suite filled with up-to-date function.

Many additions to old houses are well-executed. This master bedroom and bath addition didn't resemble the circa 1893 main house at all. Fortunately a renovation of the addition turned this architectural liability into an asset. Reworking the floor plan was the first step, moving the dressing room between the new bath space and bedroom. In the bathroom, the vanity and shower claim window-free interior walls. The claw-foot tub sits in a corner beneath windows, freeing exterior window walls for light and views.

continued

New Use, Old Piece

Remaking an antique dresser, sideboard, or table as an intriguing vanity can add one-of-a-kind charm to your bath. Here's what you need to know:

• To support a stone top, you'll need a piece that measures at least $21\frac{1}{4}$ inches deep. This allows 4 inches in front and $5\frac{1}{4}$ inches behind a 12-inch sink—a length of slab that's less likely to snap.

• If the furniture piece you are considering is too shallow, a craftsman may be able to lengthen its back and sides to support a stone surface.

• Vanities should be at least 32 to 33 inches tall. Adding bun feet can boost a piece by 2 to 3 inches.

• Allow at least 6 inches between vanity and nearby walls or fixtures for ventilation and maneuvering the piece into its site.

• Select a plain undermount or drop-in sink. It won't upstage the stone-topped furniture piece.

BEFORE

AFTER

65

A combination of modern-day function and turn-of-the-century charm makes this bath unique. The shower is roomy and modern, for example, with both a fixed faucet and handheld adjustable spray. But the sink drops into an antique dresser and the toilet is shielded from view behind an antique dressing table and a beaded-board partial wall. The tub is an old-fashioned claw foot. The dressing area and bedroom feature the same hardwood floors, but pearly gray tile takes over in the bath. Beneath it, radiant floor heating lends warmth in a way 19th-century folks couldn't even imagine. From sconces that flank mirrors to the chandelier over the tub, the light fixtures are pure period style.

1

1 From hardware and light fixtures to the tub and furnishings, the bath elements reflect the home's 1893 heritage.

2 Wallpaper revealed when a wall was torn down elsewhere in the house inspired the wallcovering choice in the bedroom.

3 In the dressing area, closet built-ins echo millwork found elsewhere in the home. The window seat bench looks like a radiator cover, but it lifts up to reveal a hamper.

2

3

Soft and Light

Pale colors in both natural and synthetic materials make this bath feel as soft as stonewashed cotton.

High gloss has no place here. Instead a galley bath with twin vanities on one side, and a toilet, tub, and shower on the other takes a softer approach. Sandblasted marble walls offer a light, comfortably worn-looking finish. Mirrors hover just in front of the wall surface, and sinks mounted to the wall float over a limestone floor. The vanities, crafted of pale yellow laminate, both contribute to the soft, sunny look and provide some budget relief.

Paired with marble tops, this coupling of materials is like wearing a finely tailored oxford shirt with a pair of jeans. Marble walls separate the toilet space, shower, and a tub across from the vanities. Each area sports its own window, and each window's value doubles in the vanity mirrors directly across the way. Aside from surface materials, this bath is free of decoration save a few well-chosen plants that add interest without clutter.

1 Wall-mounted vanities appear to float above a limestone floor, just as the mirrors seem to float over the wall surface.

2 Settled into a seafoam-green marble surround and matching flooring, the spa tub resides opposite the vanities, where window views are reflected in the mirrors.

3 The frameless glass shower door enclosure and white temperature control knobs support the hushed style of the bath.

4 A partial wall between toilet area and tub features a cutout that maintains privacy yet preserves a sense of openness. Both spaces have operable windows that bring in light, views, and fresh breezes.

Take-It-Easy Type

A successful style shift

A breezy, light, refreshing feel comes from French doors and plenty of windows in this bath.

Separated from other living spaces that are often on view, master baths have three style options: Share the home's existing style, diverge completely, or shift without shocking. Added on to a 1906 house, this bath takes the latter route. At first glance it appears clean and modern. Then you notice that the shapes and proportions of its cabinetry follow those of built-ins found elsewhere in the home. Elements are simplified: Lines are cleaner and less detailed, cabinets are white instead of stained wood, and there is plenty of brushed stainless and nickel. Still the marble countertops, reproduction fixtures, and sconce lighting in the bath relate to the home's historic period flavor. Together they make the space appear a modern cousin to the other rooms in the house.

French doors leading to a terrace and windows line all but one of the bathroom walls. Combined with crisp white curtains, tall ceilings, and a cool, white-and-aqua color scheme, an airy, refreshing ambience emerges. The angled interior walls and unusual vanity and bath positions create an interesting space and intriguing views from each part of the bath.

3

1 *The multidrawer vanity keeps clutter at bay and is a handy place to sit.*

2 *The angled placement allows improved access and views to the windows.*

3 *During the morning rush, separate vanities give a couple plenty of elbowroom. A window over one vanity boosts the room's sunlight; a mirror over the dressing table fills in for grooming needs.*

4 *An adjacent terrace just outside the bath ushers fresh breezes into the room, giving the space a beach-hotel feel. The intriguing shape comes from the out-of-the-ordinary, angled arrangement.*

4

Brand-New Character

A second-story master bath addition carries the torch for the home's 1880s architectural detail. Beneath a gabled roof and dormer windows, the built-in dressers and cabinetry, wainscoting, and crown molding do the original structure proud. Along with those luxurious details of old are a vaulted ceiling, jetted tub, separate shower, and spacious vanities and closets well suited to 21st-century living. The connection to years gone by is so strong that at first blush a visitor might not recognize this space as freshly built.

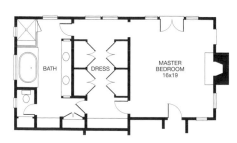

1 Beaded-board wainscoting, shutters, and ceiling panels add visual texture and detail to an otherwise vacuous space. Generous crown molding placed two-thirds up the wall helps the soaring ceilings feel spacious without becoming overwhelming.

2 Built into the hall near the closets, a dresser that mimics old-time furnishings. The wall above is mirrored and finished with wood trim.

3 Part of this master suite addition has a southwest exposure that borders on overly bright. Gray marble and pale yellow walls help calm the harsh light.

4 Vintage touches include glass knobs on the vanity drawers, beveled glass medicine cabinet mirrors, millwork trim, and old-fashioned faucets.

5 While the shower glass puts the modern-day luxury on view, the jetted, softly rounded edges recall yesteryear's claw-foot tubs.

6 The shower marble walls and a beaded-board exterior turn a shower stall into a design highlight that boosts the bathroom's spacious feel.

A Stretch Tudor

The 1920s Tudor Revival home was large and roomy, but its master bedroom's meager bath and closet (5×9-foot and 5×5-foot respectively) were not. Fortunately both were located at the home's second-story perimeter—with a breezeway adjacent on ground level. Thanks to the breezeway, the tiny bath and closet were knocked down and incorporated into a 20×17-foot bath suite addition on the second level. The presence of the breezeway eliminated a hassle common to additions, which is laying a new foundation. And as a bit of delicious icing, the new space features French doors that open to a balcony.

The bath with its jetted tub and steam shower, features up-to-the-minute modern technology, but its style honors the home's historic design. Classic pilasters and a contemporary glass block wall blend artfully with stately moldings and cultured marble surfaces.

1

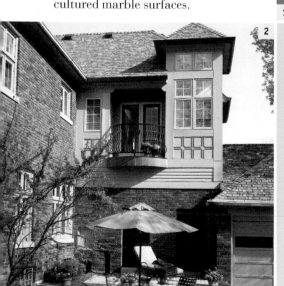

2

1 The 7-inch-thick wall behind the vanities is twice as deep as a standard wall, allowing for extra-roomy medicine cabinets.

2 The cedar-sided bath addition stretches over a brick breezeway leading from house to garage. Rooflines and architectural details were designed in keeping with the home's 1920s Tudor Revival style.

3 The two-person jetted tub fits snugly into the corner between the shower and French doors that open to the balcony. The tub surround is topped with marble and wrapped with beaded board.

4 A 6×6-foot steam shower features double showerheads and an enclosed, curved glass block wall. The steam unit is housed in a nearby linen closet and delivers extra warmth on cold mornings.

5 The new closet serves as the bath entry and buffers noise between the bathing area and the bedroom.

3

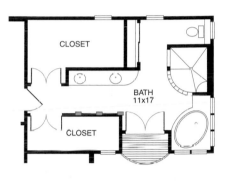

CLOSET

CLOSET

BATH
11x17

5

4

Variation on a
His-and-Hers

Bedroom moves out, bath moves in

A former farmhouse bedroom becomes a roomy master bath suite with he-wants, she-wants amenities.

Adding a bedroom to this late 1800s farmhouse was the route to gaining a master bath. The former 19×12-foot bedroom became the bath suite site. Dressed with beaded board, marble, hardwood floors, and porcelain sinks with vintage-style fittings, the new bath stays true to the home's farmhouse roots. The beauty of this bath lies in the way the homeowners took their personal style beyond the notion of double sinks.

One wanted a sink with plenty of storage, so her sink drops into a vanity, located next to a dressing table. The other had his heart set on a chunky console sink, so toiletries stash in a tall cabinet that separates a console sink from tub. Both love to soak in the tub, but when it comes to showering, one loves steam, the other enjoys elbowroom. Her small shower is equipped with a steam generator. He gave up space in the adjacent closet to get his roomy shower stall.

Both wanted an overall calming look for their bath, so they chose subdued colors and uncluttered design elements to frame to the room's window views that change with the seasons.

1 Playing off the room's beaded-board wainscoting, green and white striped wallpaper brings barely-there vertical interest to the upper walls.

2 Tall cabinets flank the tub, putting toiletries and towels within easy reach. One of the lower "drawers" is actually a tilt-out hamper.

3 White marble on her dressing table matches the top of the tub surround and sink vanity. A beaded-board panel in a bottom drawer front visually connects the dressing table to the walls and beaded-board vanity front walls. Both his big shower stall and her smaller, steam-fitted shower have tumbled marble surfaces.

4 "His" sink in this suite is an old-fashioned console with shapely legs. A tall cabinet next to the sink stores grooming supplies.

5 French doors open the bedroom-turned-bath-suite onto a private hall that leads to the new bedroom. The bath gets plenty of light from windows and doors on either end of the room and in the private hall.

3

4

5

BEFORE

MASTER BEDROOM
20x12

CLOSET

BATH

AFTER

CLOSET

BATH
19x12

HALL

CLOSET

◄ TO MASTER BEDROOM

Beaded Board

Easy-to-Do Decorative Resource

Beaded board played a starring role in the His-and-Hers with Variation bath shown on pages 76-77. Applied as wainscoting and cabinet inserts, and coated with white paint, beaded board gives the brand new bath an instant shot of old-fashioned style

Installing beaded board is a manageable project for a homeowner to do well with ordinary tools. Most install the material using panel adhesive, so no fasteners mar the surface. It's installed level with its edges hidden behind baseboard, chair rail, or crown molding, and for this reason, some think beaded board is even easier to apply than wallpaper or decorative painting.

Beaded board began appearing in homes as an architectural detail during the 17th century and was used in both formal and country cottage applications. Back then it was milled only of solid-sawn, tongue-and-groove lumber. It's still available that way, and some purists prefer the depth of the beaded detail that individual boards provide. However, most beaded board sold is offered in 4×8 sheets of hardwoods, softwoods, and medium density fiberboard (MDF). Beaded board in sheet form is less expensive, lighter weight, more uniform, and much easier and faster to install than its solid-sawn cousin. Wood-faced-beaded-board panels take stain or paint; MDF has an exceptionally smooth surface that takes paint very well. The beaded detail in the board allows you to join panels without creating noticeable seams. You'll see it on ceilings, walls, cabinet and door front inserts, and furnishings—you can even line the backs of exposed cupboards and bookcases.

Like a stripe ticking fabric, beaded boards' vertical nature makes it a crossover design element—a good bridge or mixer of styles. That means it quickly imbues a room with old-fashioned style—leaning to either a formal or country look depending on how it's used—and it also works in a contemporary setting.

Beaded board adds subtle visual texture to a room, eliminating the need for complicated decorative schemes. The ways you can use beaded board are endless, but these color scheme strategies are particularly surefire:
• White-painted beaded board paired with white-painted walls.
• White-painted beaded board with a pale to medium color on the walls.
• White-painted beaded board paired with small-scale wallpaper in pale to medium color values.
• Stained beaded board with darker hues on the walls, such as royal blue, forest green, and wine red.
• Beaded boardm that is painted in medium hues and trimmed with stained wood.

1 *Limiting color to milky hues in this attic bath lets star status go to millwork—window and cabinet trim and beaded board wainscoting—ceiling angles, hardwood floors, and a pedestal sink. The monochromatic hue is calming, not boring, thanks to the texture the millwork provides.*
2 *Beaded board serve both as architectural detail on the walls and tub surround here, and as a furniture detail in cabinet fronts. Using it both ways in the same room provides textural continuity.*
3 *The color of water, robin's eggs, and clear sky make fresh blue a lovely choice paired with milky, white-painted beaded board. Here blue walls between a beaded board ceiling and wainscoting casts a beach-fresh feel that's invigorating in a bath space. At certain times of day, light reflects the blue hue across the beaded board, adding a magical dimension to the room's color character.*

1

Beach
Sensation

As this bath shows, spaciousness is measured in more than big square footage numbers alone.

Twelve by ten feet is neither grand nor tiny when it comes to a master bath, but here it feels larger than the dimensions alone suggest. Beachy colors and a beamed skylit ceiling add to the room's sense of space, and broad rectangular windows bring in light and breezes. Jerusalem Gold marble on the bathing walls and Oasis Yellow marble on the countertop recall sand; the golden tones are supported by vanity cabinetry in a nigre veneer. Wall-mounted over a floor of glistening mosaic glass tiles, the vanity adds to the floating, beach feel of the bath. Where are the waves? Find them in the curves of the shower wall, tub surround, and mirror lighting over the vanity.

1 Despite the bath's relatively small dimensions, the shower area has room for two and is fitted with an overhead rainfall-style faucet and height-adjustable handheld spray.

2 A curved shower wall and tub surround soften the edges of intersection architecture. In laminated glass, the shower wall and toilet wall create privacy without consuming space.

3 Cut in a variety of rectangular shapes, Jerusalem Gold marble slabs form the tub and shower walls and the surround.

4 Overhead a large skylight and broad rectangular windows—one wrapping the corner— nearly eliminate the need for lights during the day.

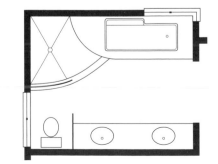

4

Short on space?

That's good news! Like gourmet cooks who find large kitchens exhausting and small ones delightfully efficient, the tight space available for a master bath may emerge as an asset rather than a liability. Using savvy strategies, you can pack loads of luxury and function into a sliver of space. Smart planning can create collision-free traffic patterns for you and your partner. One final note about small-bath appreciation: A smaller space means there is less surface to cover. In turn it means that you may be able to afford more indulgent materials that would break your budget in a larger, looser space. Turn the pages and behold some real gems.

Small
Master Baths

Furniture Style Scores
On a Curve

Compact doesn't have to mean small

The sinuous lines of the cabinetry and countertop add to the spatial efficiency and grace of this bath.

Curvaceous, furniture-quality cabinetry and a light but grounded color scheme bring high style to a 10½×8–foot master bath. The arched crown moldings, feet, and legs of the "unfitted" cabinetry create luxurious visual interest. Three stacks of upper cabinets, balanced on a foundation of two big base cabinets and a set of drawers, more than compensate for the reduced counter depth of the double vanity that protrudes in front of each sink. Reeded glass fronts on the upper cabinet doors add sparkle and further the sense of spaciousness. A roomy shower, enclosed in glass and fitted with two heads, allows for long sight lines that add to the spacious feel, while taking up less space than a tub. The caramel and chocolate-on-vanilla color scheme is particularly delicious. A brown and cream striped window blind ties it all together.

1 At the arched window next to the vanity, Roman blinds in brown and cream stripes pull up from the sill to offer privacy with a view.

2 Pewter-finish, cross-handle faucets convey vintage style.

3 Curved lines please the eye, and this double vanity has plenty. You can see curves aplenty—bowing out in the soffits above the mirrors, in the base cabinets that bear the sinks, and in the cabinet feet. Electrical outlets are hidden in the niches behind the flowers.

1

1 *Towel hooks above the toilet are easy to reach and don't interfere with the shower door. The curved glass shower stall gives an airy, wide-open feel to the space.*

2 *A white, freestanding cabinet, built with curves that echo the vanity, has room for plenty of linens. The long legs show off the floor underneath—an expanse of cream-color marble tiles with mosaics that match the brown marble of the vanity.*

Concrete with a Twist

It's not just for driveways anymore

Concrete—once synonymous with "slab" or "block"—is finally getting its due as a material capable of manifold shapes and surprising gloss.

The bold geometric shapes and colors used to decorate this 10×12-foot master bath celebrate the modern art aesthetic. The tropical mango and lime color theme is the first thing you notice, and clean-lined geometric shapes are the next. The trapezoidal vanity is crafted out of figured sycamore cabinetry with a concrete countertop and two integrated sinks.

Dye—not paint—brings the colored drawer fronts into the theme without concealing the wood grain. Stained concrete is the material of choice—for the countertop, sinks, and floor. It forms the tub surround, shower floor, and threshold as well.

In the corner an oval tub basks in light from surrounding window bank. The bath feels spacious and airy. Two circular mirrors above the vanity make the most of the light streaming through the ample windows. The edge-free glass panels of the shower surround add sparkle, giving a wide-open feel.

1 An expansion joint is structurally necessary where two concrete slabs meet. Here, the joint is curved to play up the geometrics and tangy colors.

2 A pair of circular mirrors—and a rectangular mirror to the side—serve grooming purposes while bouncing light throughout the bath.

3 Integral concrete sink fronts are cast at an angle. The move makes for bigger sinks and underscores the room's angles.

4 Unobtrusive frosted glass window panes add to tub-area privacy. The faucet and controls are positioned to allow maximum room in the oval tub.

BEFORE

AFTER

2

Clean
Getaway

Angling for more space

Walls cut across two corners of this room, enclosing the vanities and freeing up more closet and shower space.

The master bath in a West Coast contemporary home features lots of natural light—from a bank of windows mounted over the tub in addition to a full-length skylight. All that glass adds to the ambience— affording a relaxing view of the cedar and hemlock trees that surround the home. Although users can adjust the slatted blinds for complete privacy, the evergreens effectively block sight lines to adjoining homes.

The design of the room enhances the light, open treatment; a half-wall separates the deep soaking tub from the toilet area, helping the 12×17-foot room seem more spacious than it is. Gray and black tile gives way to light gray walls for a crisp, clean look that's light, yet not white-out dazzling. A natural wood color door leads to a walk-in closet that also serves as a sound buffer between the bath and a child's bedroom. "Floating" vanities and a wood frame mirror give the room a pleasing, casual look.

1 *A shaft of sunlight plays on the handsome, walnut-panel closet door, visually warming the room's cool gray-and-white color palette.*

2 *Placing the vanity within a V-shape maximizes usable space.*

3 *The room's custom vanity features two deep sink basins and a handy laundry chute between.*

4 *A spacious walk-in, double-head shower allows two to clean up simultaneously and eliminates the need for a shower door or curtain. Double exhaust fans keep steam from entering the closet area.*

3

91

1

A modest-size room seems spacious with a jetted tub, towel warmers, radiant heating, and a glass shower.

If you're stuck with a tiny bath, but are reluctant to cannibalize space from adjacent rooms to create something more livable, this two-part solution might be the answer. Bump out the space—just a little—and then make use of every square inch with efficient design and top-of-the-line amenities.

That formula transformed an 11×7-foot, garden-variety bath into this spectacular 11×7-foot haven that features a jetted tub, double vanity, a variety of storage cabinets, a marble shower, luxurious radiant-heated towel racks and floor, as well as motorized window blinds. The homeowners purchased custom components to optimize the space. For instance instead of a typical closet for towels and other bulky items, tilt-out drawers built into unused space in the tub surround store them away. In addition the sink vanity features recessed drawers and retractable light fixtures.

Together the bright white design, large windows, tall mirrors, and glass shower visually expand the modest-size bathroom. This kind of custom approach takes more time and costs more—but the payoffs are bigger too.

Small and Sumptuous

BEFORE

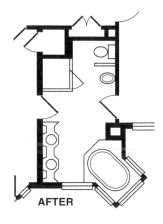

AFTER

1 The tall vanity mirrors create an illusion of space. Elegant cabinetry combines form and function. The flared-door drawers create more space between the vanity and bath. Rhinestone pulls accent plain white cabinets.

2 The bathtub niche basks in the light of three surrounding windows. The angled bump-out was built specifically to fit the tub without any wasted space.

3 The 38×38-inch shower stall opposite the tub is outfitted with sleek fixtures and creamy white granite tile. The glass enclosure keeps sight lines open.

4 Efficient elegance extends to lighting and storage. False door fronts above the medicine cabinet conceal retractable lights that illuminate the nearby mirror.

5 Tilt-out drawers take advantage of the unused space beneath the tub.

Under the Eaves

No need to raise the roof
The attics in many vintage homes are secluded baths or master suites just waiting to be discovered.

at arm's length. Prescription medicines and other items find a place in the drawers of the linen cabinet beside the tub.

Sometimes it's possible to add a master suite without altering a home's footprint or floor plan. The suite in this 1917 Craftsman-style home, for example, was installed in the attic. Old-house renovators often discover extra space in this area, where the angled roof ceiling meets the vertical walls. Here the knee wall was pushed back about a foot, making room for a deck-mounted whirlpool tub and its mechanicals.

Space-saving, vintage-style pedestal sinks are backed with beaded wainscoting made of tongue-and-groove 1×4s. These boards offer a much deeper detail (and more authentic vintage appeal) than milled beaded-board panels. Instead of medicine cabinets, ledges beneath the two oval mirrors keep toiletries

1 Thanks to careful design and a top-floor location, this diminutive bath has room for a spacious shower and large whirlpool tub. The secret is a skylight above the tub that raises the low ceiling, adding headroom, light and a sky's-the-limit sense of space.
2 The vintage tile around the tub features two hands of an Art Deco relief design.
3 Chrome-and-porcelain faucets add to the old-time atmosphere, as does sconce lighting over the sinks.

Craftsman
Class

More authentic than original

Formerly neglected utility rooms, the baths in old houses deserve a shining update.

Bathrooms in early-20th century houses are usually spartan at best. But if you're stuck with a room that's all function and no style, you can remodel it to complement the style of the rest of the house. This bath in a 1917 Craftsman home is a case in point. Before the bath was remodeled, the door opened directly onto the toilet, with a sink and a dated tub/shower unit just beyond. To create the characteristic Craftsman warmth and drama, the original bath was gutted. Plumbing was reconfigured to accommodate a more welcoming layout with vanities to the right, a custom storage unit to the left, and a commode, which is tucked behind a short divider.

The star of the bath is the double shower. Framed with fir— stained to match the woodwork in the rest of the house— the shower flaunts Craftsman-style tile that is accented with randomly arranged tiles with a raised pinecone motif. Separate on/off and temperature controls for showerheads on facing walls allow for individual preset temperature settings. Other added touches include wainscoting, period lighting, a laundry chute, and a glass shower door.

1 Stained-fir woodwork and period-style tile in this family bath reinforce a Craftsman theme found throughout the house.

2 Handmade pottery sinks with vintage-style brushed nickel fixtures sit in a furniture-style wood counter with a waterproof, high-gloss finish that wipes clean.

Radiator Redux

Don't let a massive radiator intrude on your bath's style. In this bath the wall unit opposite the sinks was custom-designed to conceal a radiator behind a mesh screen and towel bar. Added benefits include a warm towel when you step out of the bath or shower and radiators enclosed in cabinetry—making them more efficient and effective. Here's why: The air warmed by uncovered radiators rises in columns behind the units and gathers at the ceiling. With the aid of vented cabinets—often lined with heat-reflecting galvanized sheet metal—heat is pushed out into the room.

1

Thrills without Frills

"Clean and contemporary" is a particularly apt phrase—and style—when applied to a bath.

If you find traditional styles somewhat elaborate for your taste, contemporary design offers a refreshingly cool change. The streamlined style is particularly appropriate for bathrooms, where easy-to-clean functionality and a fresh, modern look go hand in hand. This room, for example, has a spare, contemporary look without being dated or sterile. That's because the surfaces used—wood, glass, granite, and stainless steel—are familiar choices that have been transformed into an exotic, high-energy tableau.

The first turn away from the ordinary is taken in the form of a set of red-stained drawers. The color—an aniline-dyed version of the naturally blond ash cabinetry flanking the vanity—makes a bold statement, warming up the green tones in the vanity countertop. The tub and shower areas are similarly bold and clean. A pure white whirlpool tub sits on the curved, black granite-covered platform, which sweeps into the adjacent shower enclosure and becomes a convenient bench platform. The open shower is set off by unframed glass doors and a nearly invisible glass divider separating it from the tub. The faucets, hardware, and stainless-steel accents further the sleek and simple look. The result is a smooth, high-contrast bath—intentionally short on frippery and frills.

2

BATH
9x11

CLOSET

1 *The elevated tub rises to the view, while the granite surround offers seating and storage for both the tub and shower. Sunlight pours through the glass divider.*

2 *White walls offer a clean backdrop to the dramatic color scheme. The granite-topped double vanity features a splash of color with ash cabinetry dyed red. It gracefully combines nature's metal, wood, and stone.*

The Amenity of
Serenity

Composed of top-notch materials and a
few well-chosen elements, this bath
attains a gallerylike feel.

Does your current bath neglect a beautiful view? This Florida beach house bath achieves a breezy, serene feel you can re-create in any site where there is light, privacy, and—most important—something beyond the windows that's a pleasure to behold. Its simple, dramatic approach showcases two features: floor-to-ceiling windows—and their picturesque view—and a vintage-style soaking tub. Crisp white objects predominate here—from porcelain fixtures to the whitewashed vanity to the graceful cotton-duck drapes that puddle on the floor. The room feels at once starkly clean and warmly romantic. The freestanding tub and custom vanity decorate the space like carefully placed furnishings rather than permanent necessities. An unframed oval mirror and two modest sconces complement the vanity without overpowering its clean Shaker style. An oversize framed mirror beside the tub provides a silvery element of glamour. Set on the Phillipine shell-stone tile floor to lean, rather than hang, the huge mirror lends casual grandeur while reflecting the abundant light.

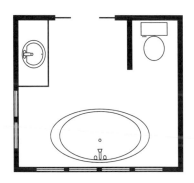

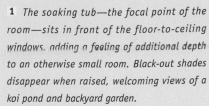

1 The soaking tub—the focal point of the room—sits in front of the floor-to-ceiling windows, adding a feeling of additional depth to an otherwise small room. Black-out shades disappear when raised, welcoming views of a koi pond and backyard garden.

2 This whitewashed Shaker-style table looks like an antique that was converted to a vanity, but it was custom-made for this room. A surface-mounted vessel sink echoes the freestanding soaking tub.

3 An oversize antique mirror brightens the room and visually opens the confined space. Reproduction shower hooks with cut-glass knobs add to the room's casual, romantic feel.

4 A vintage-style cut-glass door handle sets the tone for the entire room when the pocket door is opened or closed.

5 Faucets, hot and cold water knobs, and a telephone-style hand shower are pedestal-mounted outside the tub, giving more space to relax and unwind in the deep tub.

2

3

4

5

Less Isn't Less

What do you want most in YOUR bath?
Setting clear priorities was key to getting the most out of the least in this deluxe bath. Upgraded materials help.

Livable, luxurious bathrooms come in all sizes—including very small. Extra space is nice, but getting the amenities you want is more important. If you're hemmed in, the goal is to find a way to pamper yourself within the bounds of the space you have. In doing so you'll find that small baths have an advantage over larger rooms when it comes to remodeling: They require fewer materials, thus allowing you to splurge on quality and good design.

The priority in renovating this 10×5-foot master bath in a vintage home was to incorporate a two-person whirlpool tub and a decent-size shower without a cramped feel. In order to do this, the builders annexed an adjacent hall closet, gutted the original bath, and moved the entry closer to the vanity wall to make way for larger, more luxurious amenities. The vanity counter narrowed to accommodate the new door placement; it bows out, but only around the sink. A compact whirlpool tub (imported from France, where smaller baths are readily available) and a generously proportioned shower fit comfortably. The glass shower door and walls stop short of the ceiling, creating a looser space. Neutral color limestone tilework accented with tumbled marble renders the small space a rich yet restful environment.

1

2

1 The muted color combination creates a relaxing atmosphere. High-end materials, such as limestone tile, a custom-crafted mural-like floor, and decorative molding belie the small stature of the room.

2 Tumbled marble in various shades of brown and beige are inset in limestone to give the room a subtle yet highly decorative focus.

3 This extra-deep, two-person French whirlpool takes up less room than domestic models. It rests in the space that was gained by annexing both a hall and bathroom closet.

4 The curved bump-out of the sink area helps to smooth the otherwise sharp lines of the vanity.

3

4

The list of specialized baths outlined in this book might suggest that every home is filled with bathrooms for specific users: master baths, guest baths, kids' baths, and powder rooms. But many rely on family baths to serve various combinations of family members and guests. Small or large, simple or lavish, these multipurpose baths work hard to keep their users comfortable, clean, and refreshed. These baths deserve as much consideration as any other in the home. Browse here for some well-executed examples.

Family
Baths

Universal Design to Grow On

Designed from scratch to be wheelchair accessible, this bath is also a handsome addition to a vintage home.

This spacious 21×7-foot bath in a 1930s home was custom-designed for the owner's preteen son, who uses a wheelchair. The room is divided into three sections: shower, toilet and vanity, and bath. The entire room is designed to serve its user as he grows into adulthood.

From top to bottom and side to side, the space is designed without thresholds and other impediments to a wheelchair user. Tile patterns were chosen both for their classic cheer and their ability to blend with the home's vintage roots. Hexagonal floor tiles are slip-resistant too. Three windows—two in glass block for privacy—wash the room in light. The whole space is safe, easy to use, and welcoming. Awesome, in the words of its user!

BATH
21x7

1

1 This wheelchair-accessible bath features a shower with a wide doorway, a sink without a base cabinet, and a whirlpool tub with a wide ledge.
2 There's plenty of approach-and-turn room in the tub, toilet, and vanity area.
3 A freestanding shower bench offers more flexibility than a fixed built-in. Large faucet handles here and at the vanity are easy to grasp.
4 Colorful tile patterns and a chartreuse chest of drawers give the bath some zip and personality.

2

3

Universal Notes

Several features of this universal design bath will provide for the child users as they grows and their needs change.

• Structural supports in the ceiling. For the future installation of an electric lift that helps the user get in and out of the tub.

• The absence of closets and built-in storage for maximum floor space. Rather than locking into a fixed-closet scenario, homeowners can purchase freestanding furnishings and arrange them as needs change.

• Looped support bars at the toilet. These offer an upper and lower handle for a user whose height will be increasing.

• An adjustable mirror to accommodate height change.

• A showerhead that adjusts for height along a vertical bar.

1 *Creamy white tiles in a variety of shapes combine with lively patterns in gray, blue, and black. The result: a cheerful bath space that will suit the user throughout life. Bars flanking the toilet hang flat against the wall when not in use.*

2 *The sink rim juts out past the countertop, making it more accessible to someone who's seated. Similarly, the drain is at the back corner of the sink so the pipes below are out of the way of a wheelchair user.*

3 *One end of the tub narrows to fit in next to the toilet, the other broadens to serve as a bench—helpful in getting in and out of the tub.*

4 *A crank-operated pulley system tilts the mirror to serve someone in a seated position.*

2

3 4

A Honey of a Bath

Golden hues in wood and stone, sunshine-yellow walls, and glossy white tile combine for a cheerful look that's lively and rich with timeless detail.

Fanciful cutouts in the fascia set the tone in this bath, specially designed for a family with young children. The lighthearted ambience and orderly arrangement is grounded in beautiful materials that include a furniture-like double vanity, glossy white tile with detail pieces, a stained-glass window, and a heated travertine floor with a braided mosaic tile border. Two sinks and plenty of vanity storage help the family move through their morning routine. A deep ledge at one end of the bath aids a parent who is helping a child out of the bath. Warm-tone surfaces are a good backdrop for the kinds of colorful accessories kids enjoy, and they work equally well with the muted-hue linens adults often favor. The beauty of this bath is its timeless cheerful quality, which is as appealing to a youngster as to an adult. Everywhere your eye goes, it's rewarded with a visual detail to savor.

1

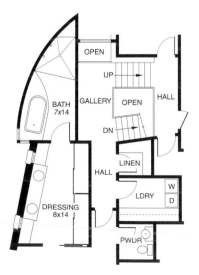

2

1 A heating system beneath the golden travertine floor adds real warmth to the floor's warm appearance. A braided mosaic border, lovely in its own right, draws the eye to the Travertine good looks.

2 Two sinks and a long, low countertop help a family speed through its morning routine.

3 Finished with a multicolor, striated wash, the furniture-style vanity is an intriguing piece to behold. The upper cabinets tango with glossy white tile to frame the mirror and form a backsplash.

Mundane to Marvelous

Detail does it

A vivid hue and pretty tiles rescue this
ordinary bath from a plain existence.

1

Ignoring the conventional belief that a pocket-size space should be decorated simply, this 9×6½-foot bath went from small to smashing thanks largely to decorative tile. Tile comes in a vast assortment of colors and patterns, and it's often packaged into "collections" that make it easy to choose coordinating accents. In this case inexpensive white tiles cover the vanity counter, walls, and floor; more expensive hand-painted tiles frame the vanity mirror and shower window. Mottled cobalt blue matte-finish tiles randomly set with decorative tiles featuring frogs, fish, turtles, and dragonflies cover the shower surround. The top drawer of the inexpensive stock vanity was replaced with wood to support an exciting tile border. The broad vanity mirror and the glass shower door visually expand the tiny bathroom space, as does the mottled, undulating color in the tile: Instead of stopping the eye, the watery look suggests that you can see—or swim—right through it.

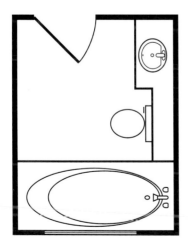

1 A soap holder featuring a playful frog-and-dragonfly pond scene punctuates the undulating field of blue shower tiles.
2 Vanity faces rarely receive special treatment. This one does; relief tiles depicting leaves and critters make a border beneath the countertop trim tiles.
3 Walls of blue tile accented with milky white imbue this small bath with big style. Trim tiles of blue and white leaves rim the inset mirror over the vanity and the glassblock window in the shower. The blue tile shower surround is "crawling" with randomly placed critter tiles.

2

Guest baths are a special case. Depending on your lifestyle, the guest bathroom may be used only a few nights a year by the same visiting relatives or almost constantly by lots of people of all ages. Approaches to building or reworking a guest bath are similarly varied. If the bath gets light use by special people on special occasions, you may want to focus on lavish materials and finishes such as glass countertops and polished-metal fixtures. Or perhaps you'd like to create a bath that reflects the taste or personality of a frequent guest. Then again, you may decide that a bath so seldom used is best freshened with a little cash and a lot of flair, sparing your budget for expenditures on more often-used rooms. The choices are yours, and you'll find lots of inspiring ideas here.

Guest
Bath

Arts and Crafts for
Visitors

An earthy option

Tiled surfaces, natural-finish hardwood, rectangular shapes, and wrought-iron hardware characterize the style.

Earthy hues, simple woodwork, and a balanced design create a warm Craftsman-theme setting in this straightforward yet luxurious guest bath. The look starts with cherry cabinetry, designed with recessed panels and wrought-iron hardware. Over the vanity, Craftsman-style wall lamps flank a mirrored medicine cabinet. Three slate tile arrangements provide interest and texture in harmonious colors. The primary slate floor features copper insets and underfloor radiant heat that warms bare feet on chilly mornings. The treetop location of the bath means there's not much call for window coverings. When needed, honeycomb blinds drop from the casement window tops.

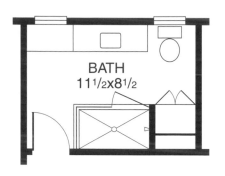

1

BATH
11½x8½

1 *Enclosing a former deck on the upper story made room for this guest bath.*

2 *An edge-free glass shower surround makes the bath feel more roomy; here, it also allows a full view of the treetops from the shower. The shower wall slate tiles are installed on the diagonal for visual interest. Those on the floor are smaller and laid parallel with the walls. Guests can find extra towels, blankets, and bedding in the floor-to-ceiling linen closet.*

3 *Flanking the vanity with a window seat and toilet creates a well-balanced wall arrangement that complements the symmetry of the Arts and Crafts style. The casement window muntins reflect the style as well.*

4 *Two storage drawers tucked under the window seat put every inch of space to work. Built-ins such as the window seat are a common Arts and Crafts feature.*

3

4

Smart
Luxury

Small in space, rich in custom detail
Remodeled within the same space, this
small bath grew in style and function.

An ordinary 7$\frac{1}{2}$×11–foot bathroom boosted its ability to please with a few clever tricks—and a fresh dressing of opulent materials. The removal of a privacy wall between the toilet and vanity expanded the space visually and made room for a bigger vanity. Replacing the standard tub/shower/sliding glass door ensemble with a curtained shower stall also broke down barriers. White beaded-board cabinetry topped with travertine tile (also used in varying patterns on the floor and in the shower) finds a complementary partnership in brushed nickel fixtures and knobs. The travertine texture feels soft to hands and feet. Two more cabinets and a set of drawers tuck into a closet with sliding doors, adding yet another dimension.

BATH
7$\frac{1}{2}$x11

1 Standard sink faucet spouts failed to reach far enough over the broad border of this custom tiled sink, but a tub faucet works perfectly.

2 Mounting the vanity sink to the left made room for a vertical row of drawers to the right. The vanity stands at kitchen-counter height to reduce stooping and allow for deeper drawers.

3 A deep shower clad in travertine tile took the place of a standard tub/shower enclosure. A built-in niche holds shower supplies. This bathroom feels spacious thanks to an off-white, monochromatic scheme. A variety of surface textures gives the room plenty of visual interest.

4 Cabinetry and counter treatments continue into the closet so this space looks terrific whether closet doors are open (left) or closed (right). Louvered, bypass sliding doors are sturdier and take up less space than bifold doors do.

Mannered and
Masculine

Mahogany, marble, and shimmering tile create a warm and masculine aura in this bath. Although the remodeled room is relatively small, it includes all the amenities a guest could want or need. The custom sink vanity—built of rich mahogany and a wine-color marble—extends from the wall, yet gives the pedestal-style sink an open look. The vanity offers ample space for toiletries as does a 5-inch-deep ledge at the base of the mirror. A medicine cabinet hangs above the toilet.

The glass shower door, trimmed with brass, also serves as a steam room. Covered with metallic-look ceramic tiles, the interior walls reflect a rainbow of shimmering color. A marble bench invites your guest to sit back and soak up the steam.

The lighting is soft and muted overall, thanks to uplighting installed in the ceiling molding. Double sconces on either side of the vanity provide task lighting when deeper reflection is in order.

1 Plumbing lines hide behind wooden panels under the custom vanity. Sconces enhance the tailored appearance. The iridescent finish on the shower tiles lends intrigue. When the light changes, the tiles appear to shift color.

2 The woodwork and custom cabinetry are mahogany. The vented cabinet beneath the window conceals the radiator. A marble floor creates an air of elegance and sophistication.

3 The steam shower glass walls render it nearly invisible. Brass fixtures paired with shiny tiles provide a soothing golden glow.

Small Spaces

Inventive design and a host of new space-saving products can help you install a number of bathroom amenities in less space than you may have thought possible. Here are some ideas to consider as you ponder building or remodeling your gem of a guest bathroom:

• **A frameless glass shower surround.** These nearly invisible enclosures allow you to add a shower stall without appearing to take up any space at all. Unless daily cleaning is a plus in your book, you'll want to avoid installing glass stalls in high-use bathrooms; the glass readily reveals soap scum, water deposits, and even fingerprints. Even so, they work beautifully in small baths that are rarely used. Take this tip: Use the same wall and floor treatments inside and outside the shower for a flowing, seamless look.

• **Smoke and mirrors.** Forget the smoke, but use the mirrors to make small spaces live larger—the reflective quality of mirrors works magic in the confines of a cramped bath. This ingenious medicine cabinet is mirrored both inside and out. Closed, the mirror reflects a straightforward view of your face. Open, mirrors on the door's inner surfaces team up with a third mirror at the back of the cabinet to create a three-way view. A close-up magnifying mirror brings the views into the "fourth" dimension.

• **Play the angles.** Another way to visually "grow" a small space is with graphics. Diagonals, for instance, allow you to create a longer line in a small room than you can achieve with a horizontal or vertical.

• **Shrink the essentials.** By installing smaller sinks and showers in corners, you can preserve function while maintaining style.

1

1 Clear glass walls and a frameless glass door are one way to keep your shower stall from taking a visual bite out of your bathroom square footage—and to show off its handsome tilework and fixtures.

2 Diagonal lines define the shower door and mirror and add interest to the floor's colorful border of ceramic tile. Accent tiles in the shower continue the diagonal theme.

3 A diminutive stainless-steel sink tucks into a corner between the toilet and the narrow cabinet.

4 The vanity is designed with a narrow depth, which helps free up space in this bathroom. A mirrored wall instantly doubles the visual space of any bath—and lightens the room as well.

123

From Tiny to Terrific

This 9×5-foot cubicle of a bath gained a tiny foot in its remodeling, but thanks to clever design choices, all the necessities fit.

As a minor rework of this bath proves that a little more room can mean a lot more function. By stealing only a foot of space from a nearby shower, enough room was freed for a shower/tub combination with an angled glass enclosure.

Dressed with nickel-plate fixtures and a green ribbon of handmade tiles, the shower decor matches that of the rest of the room. An adjacent tower of built-in shelves stores towels and linens and affords the bath a freestanding washbasin, lending the room an additional feeling of spaciousness. The basin's nickel-plate faucet, like that of the shower, reflects the vintage flavor found in the rest of the house. Best of all: The bath packs all the function a guest could want!

1 *Since it's less expensive to move a non-loadbearing wall than it is to move plumbing fixtures, this bath retained the original positions of sink, toilet, and bathing area.*

2 *Fitted with a frameless glass door and tile that matches the rest of the room, the shower takes up less visual space than would a tub with a shower curtain. The angled-door design allows for a slim built-in cabinet and shelves.*

3 *The open-stand washbasin eliminates vanity storage possibilities but adds a vintage feel and takes up less visual space than other arrangements. The glass shelf over the sink keeps often-used toiletries within reach.*

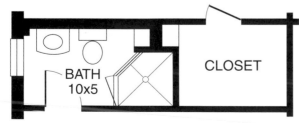

BATH 10x5

CLOSET

Trading on Texture

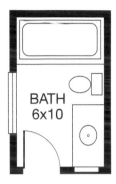

BATH
6x10

Originally the sole distinguishing feature of this 5×10-foot box of a bath was its window. An artful redo proves that warm colors, furniture-like refinement, and rich textures work their magic even in the tiniest of spaces.

The bath was originally part of the servant's quarters in a 1920s house. The owners took measures to preserve the historic home's layout, even as they sought to make the servant wing—now a guest suite— more elegant and welcoming. They also wished to merge old and new styles, retaining at least some of the home's bygone character.

The cherry vanity, wood-frame mirror, and built-in wall shelves are dressy pieces that look at home in a traditional setting.

Shiny metallic finishes on the sink, faucets, and fittings reflect the elegant excesses of the Roaring Twenties. The stunning tile treatment of the tub area, however, is colorfully contemporary. Golden crackle-finish tiles extend from floor to ceiling. A dramatic backlit niche over the tub is a calculated focal point, drawing attention away from the room's boxy dimensions.

1 *Like matted artwork, the tiled tub niche gains visual impact from its wide white border. The terra-cotta flooring is a good match for the crackle-finish wall tiles.*

2 *Open storage in the bottom half of the cherry vanity eliminates the doors and drawers that can clutter and close off a small bath. Silver bands on the mirror shine like the nickel sink and wall-hung faucet.*

At your Service

8×10 is plenty big enough

Call it eye candy, call it slight of hand: Make up for tight quarters by charming your guests with visual treats and they'll never notice the space limitations.

If you have only a tiny bath to offer your guests, don't despair—plenty of homeowners are in the same position. Display your gracious nature by dressing the room to provide both amenities and entertaining style. This tiny former servant's bedroom in a 1920s manor house was transformed into a bath in which any guest would delight. Historic colors, dramatic materials, and interesting accessories make this 8×10-foot space a surprisingly rich offering.

The color scheme features an unusual combination of warm yellow, slate blue, taupe, and brown—drawn together with black

and mahogany accents. One corner of the room features a space-saving circular shower, which is wrapped in a brown curtain whose cutouts provide a peek at its turquoise liner.

The room's only window is dressed in one-of-a-kind shutters made from an array of 19th-century glass travel slides, leaded glass, and stained glass.

1 The shower serves as a balancing focal point, and, as a freestanding piece, saves a lot of space. A centered sunflower spray head adds to the design's symmetry.

2 The room's single window provides natural light. An artist custom-made the shutters, which feature 19th-century glass slides.

3 The black ash vanity topped with a porcelain bowl grounds the room and lends it and elegant, historic focal point.

3

Creative solutions fuel the design for a
full-featured bath in a wedge of space
beneath a steeply pitched roof.

The Greenhouse Effect

Guest rooms often squeeze into
attic spaces or shed-dormer
additions that have little space for a
bathroom. This 6×11-foot bath with
a steeply sloping ceiling avoids
claustrophobia by flooding the area
with diffuse daylight.

The room's ceiling is made of
light-filtering panels that feature an
insulating fiberglass core sandwiched
in solid yet translucent fiberglass.
The panels' insulating properties are
impressive: They filter light and
provide privacy while preventing
excessive heat buildup during sunny
days and heat loss on cool nights. A
steel grid supports the panels.

Although the high-tech house
uses a lot of industrial-strength glass
and steel, the bathroom includes
organic materials that soften its high
ceilings. Travertine marble, with its
natural variations and fissures,
covers the floor, shower, and
backsplash. The stone's light color
and glossy surface brightens the
room at night.

A nearly invisible clear-glass
shower partition limits visual
barriers so the room feels like one
open area. Without blocking the
flow, a steel I-beam roof support
divides the custom vanity's polished-
granite countertop into sink and
surface areas. Streamlined hardware
and carefully edited accessories
contribute to the clean lines.

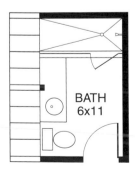

BATH
6x11

1 The vanity's countertop mirror is a must because the steep roof slope doesn't lend itself to
a mounted mirror.

2 A second mirror to the left of the towel bars is just a 180-degree turn away from the
vanity on the opposite side. Track lighting runs along the steel I-beam; half-moon sconces
provide overall illumination at night.

3 Tucked under a steeply sloping roof made of translucent fiberglass panels, this bath
dwells in a modern home that features industrial materials and geometric shapes.

Paradox prevails in the powder room. It's the tiniest room in your house, yet almost every guest and family member visits it. From a functional perspective, powder rooms should have a sink, toilet, privacy, and an ample supply of cleanup supplies within arm's reach. That's easily done in a small space.

The task is more challenging if you want the powder room to be handicap accessible (see the guidelines on pages 180–181 and the powder room on page 134). You won't need much space to accomplish a universal design, just more attention to planning. Make sure that doors are 36 inches wide and open out of the way, floors are easy to roll across, faucet handles are easy to operate, and finally, that there's enough room to transfer from chair to toilet to the sink.

The tiny, closed-door nature of powder rooms is exactly what makes them fun to decorate. Behind the powder room door, a homeowner can indulge in decorative drama, humor, color, and themes that are bold, intense, or unrelated to a home's other, more public rooms. That's the luxury of a powder room. Let the ones you see here inspire you to do yours your way.

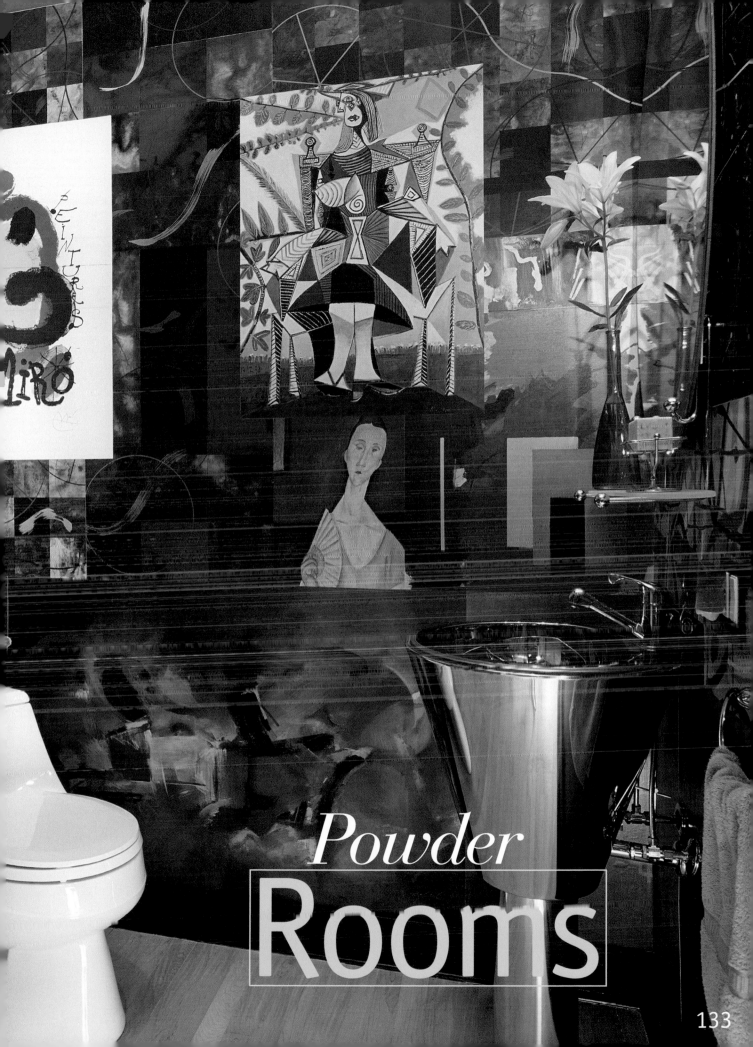

Powder
Rooms

A Beauty to Behold

Visible from nearly every room on the first floor and all this home's entries, this powder room remodel was fueled by the demand that the finished powder room would open onto something other than the toilet or a blank wall. Working with that premise, the room was designed to open onto a bun-foot vanity nestled under a drywall arch. A mirror fills the arched space behind the sink. For a dazzling effect, the arch is crowned with hand-painted morning glory vine and hummingbirds.

Despite the powder room's decorative glory, it's not large. Measuring only $6\frac{1}{2} \times 6\frac{1}{2}$ feet, its square dimensions allow for positioning the vanity and toilet opposite each other for ease and privacy.

This powder room's universal design is not so obvious to the onlooker—but the home-owning family appreciates it very much. They plan to live in the house for many years, and their parents have already

spent time here in wheelchairs.

The powder room door is 3 feet wide and hinged to swing away from the toilet. Once the door is open, the path is clear. Wheels roll smoothly across the tile floor. The linen closet door opens to the adjacent wall so that its contents are easily accessed.

1 *Dropped into a durable, solid-surface counter, a fluted oval sink and polished brass faucets with easy-to-use lever handles offer appealing detail.*

2 *Beneath an arched headdress painted with a vine and hummingbirds, the vanity's sage color and bun feet give it a furniture feel. Underfoot, the look of blue-green ceramic floor tiles flecked with brown and gold changes with the light.*

Take Note

When faced with a very visible powder room, such as this one, it is tempting to load it with high-end luxury elements. However, the styling in this room is elegantly simple. Its most notable features are its vanity-first arrangement, the arch topper above the vanity, and the decorative painting that crowns it. You can hire a decorative painter, enlist a talented friend, or purchase stencil packages to achieve a similar effect. This powder room incorporates a high-end, solid-surface countertop, fluted sink, and a bun-foot vanity; it wouldn't have nearly as much charm if it was outfitted with a plain laminate counter, simple sink, and a standard, built-in vanity.

135

Shared Space

Powder and Laundry Combos

Funny how a few square feet of centrally located main floor space becomes hot property. The pretty powder room (to make guests comfortable and spare them from private family spaces) meets its competition in the form of a dreamed of easy-access, laundry center. Good arguments exist on both sides when there's not enough room for both—and in older homes there usually isn't. The key is to take your parents' advice: Mind your manners and share the space. Solutions exist; you can find the right one on these pages.

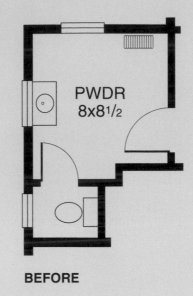

PWDR
8x8½

BEFORE

1

PWDR
8x8½

D W

AFTER

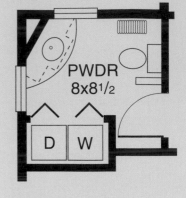

2

Functionally Fit

When a standard side-by-side washer and dryer set is too big, don't despair. You have options, and as consumers ask for products that can squeeze into tight quarters (including vacation homes and secondary locations, more appear on the market each year. You'll find the following on showroom floors now:

• Narrow, stackable washer/dryer combos in 24-inch widths require less floor space than standard side-by-side, 30-inch models.

• Tuck-under washers and dryers fit underneath a standard counter. Available in standard widths, these front-loading appliances have controls on the front panels. You can also stack them.

• Condensation dryers make it possible to install appliances in rooms and closets without venting them to the outdoors. The dryer discharges moisture into the washer's drain line.

• Cabinet-topped dryers make room for many levels of air drying on top of the appliance surface, eliminating the closet-laundry conundrum of finding a place to lay or hang just-washed delicates to dry.

3

1 In the slightly oversize powder room of an older home, the toilet compartment was swapped for a washer-dryer closet. With the toilet relocated across the room, a half-wall that screens it from the door and a working lock ensures privacy.

2 A sink snugs into the corner under a mirror that's mounted on an angle. A raisin-color vanity (made of three standard rectangular boxes) supports the crescent-shape granite top.

3 Laundry appliances and supplies tuck into a closet behind bifold doors painted to match the walls and cabinetry. The location right off the kitchen makes it easy to throw in a load of wash in between other household chores.

4 Beneath a glossy tiled counter, bifold doors with faucet-style handles swing back to reveal a front-loading washer and dryer. Upper cabinets store supplies; folded laundry stacks on the counter.

5 Reflective white tiles with black accents keep the small bath looking light and crisp. Hand towels can hang from the horizontal bars of the polished chrome sink frame.

137

Powder Room Review

The brilliance of a powder room can be easily conveyed in a photograph or two. To give you as many style and arrangement ideas as possible, the next four pages showcase an assortment of powder rooms. Browse, ponder, and let your imagination go!

Basket Case

A wooden basket once used to carry freshly harvested olives from French groves is creatively used as the vanity pedestal. The homeowners found the basket in a French antique store. Their contractor sliced slats off the back to fit around the plumbing and neatly against the wall. Topped with a creamy marble counter, the rough-hewn nature of the basket is a warm, textural counterpoint to the shiny black marble flooring underneath. The toile-covered walls and window valance act as a bridge between the light and dark marble.

Eureka!

Mining for a site near the kitchen for a powder room, this sliver turned up from a chimney-bearing closet. With the chimney relocated, beaded-board half-walls and glowing gold-painted walls moved in to set the tone of the new room. A stainless-steel sink backs into a wall niche that's topped with an arch, an architectural detail echoed in other parts of the house. Beneath a black solid-surface counter, a slim brushed steel rod stretches across the niche to hold a hand towel.

Stripes Away

This homeowner garnered an old-world look for her powder room despite an existing laminate cabinet and yellow sink that looked too new. By creating a color scheme that incorporated and/or ignored those items, she was able to get the desired look. The bathroom already had impressive moldings, an old-fashioned mirrored medicine cabinet, and a nifty tilt-in window—all of which were dressed up with coats of white paint. But the full credit for the new look goes to the walls, where the hand-painted gold stripes glow in the light with an ever-changing, aged appearance.

139

Bold and Blocky

Cut-up maple pieces assembled on the wall using thin metal strips (the kind used to divide carpet from tile flooring) creates bold style in a 4×6-foot powder room. The maple wall pays tribute to artist Piet Mondrian, who designed the image in the framed poster. A horizontal maple strip also crosses the brick-color wall, leading the eye to the toilet paper roll. A super contemporary faucet lets water flow into a frosted glass bowl perched atop nothing more than its plumbing for a thoroughly modern look.

Jewel Box

Gold-leaf wallpaper overglazed with a golden wash transforms a plain white powder room from ordinary to extraordinary. Nearly every surface is covered with gold or silver leaf. Near the cove molding a celestial-theme frieze outlines the perimeter of the room. The ceiling fixture is shaped to resemble the sun, and star-covered sconces light both sides of the mirror.

Asian Angle

Striking shapes, rich textures, and sharp design create Asian-style serenity in this 5×6-foot powder room. A bronze basin and angled limestone counter combine with grass-cloth wallcovering, a maple cabinet and flooring, and minimalist fixtures for an aesthetically pleasing balance between warm and cool. Storage happens in a cube-on-cube style wall-mount cupboard. Try to decide which element in this bathroom claims star status.

141

Adults may see it as a space for retreating and unwinding, but children see the bathroom as a place to play. The bathtub is filled with toys, after all, and the mirrors are great for making silly faces. A spunky bath that suits their bright-eyed personalities is another reason they'll succumb to the necessary brushing of teeth. You'll have less trouble getting them into the bathroom, though some convincing may be required to get them out.

Kids'
Baths

This bath was designed primarily for efficiency and ease of cleaning, but it also turned out handsomely.

Locker Room
Uptown Style

When five boys share a bath, efficiency is the name of the game. In this case a wide-open, locker room-style design suits that need. However, the homeowners shunned the standard school look that usually comes with it. Warm wood cabinetry with sparkling knobs and recessed panels are topped with deep green, durable, solid-surfacing countertops, establishing a classic look. Around the tub, shower, and backsplash, white tiles set off with black and gray create interest. The smart pocket door prevents surprise bangs in the face as kids move in and out during the morning rush!

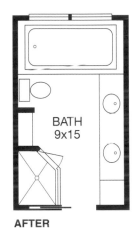

2

BATH
9x5

BATH
9x15

BEFORE

AFTER

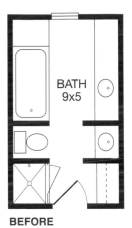

1

1 Filled with two sinks and plenty of space between them, the stretch of counter can handle three at the mirror. The cabinets below swallow a huge stash of supplies and towels. Black and gray tile patterns are energizing against white.

2 Tucking the bath under the eaves, dropping room dividers, and reworking the shower entry keep this bath for five boys from becoming an obstacle course.

3 A niche just outside the shower features a bench plus shelves, hooks, and locker room-style baskets for towels, robes, and toys.

4 Rich wood tones from the cabinetry and floor and deep green surfaces create a fresh, woodsy space. The white ceiling and walls give the sloping ceiling a visual lift.

3

4

Go Wild
West

Cowboy theme designed for trio of boys.
In this house the admonition "Go West,
young man," is a suggestion to make a
trip to the bathroom.

For a trio of boys who enjoy tales of cowboys and the Wild West, a Western theme is a logical choice for their bath. Decorative touches followed functional moves, the first of which was to lasso an adjacent bedroom closet into the bathroom space. Doing so allowed for two distinct areas: one with two sinks for general grooming, another one with more privacy for the toilet and tub/shower. Cabinetry, countertops, and fixtures boast the ability to withstand the wear and tear the boys dish out. The bath appeals to cowboy-wannabes of all ages and will hold up even when boys turn to men. But if desired, a quick change of accessories—the star, the horseshoe, the model cars—will cast a fresh, more mature mood.

BATH
7¹/₂x8

BEFORE

1

2

1

1 Handprints on backsplash tiles let the kids literally put their stamp on the bath. Durable, easy-clean, solid-surfacing forms the countertop and integral sinks.

2 Unobtrusive pullout steps at the vanity's toe kick give little folks that little extra they need. Dark knobs blend in with dark cabinets. The floor that looks like whitewashed pine is actually practical ceramic tile.

3 A navy base cabinet hides fingerprints and dings; natural maple medicine cabinets keep the look from going too dark. Peg trim makes towel hang-up a cinch, while a display ledge backed by beaded board and a lighted star indulge collections.

4 Borrowing space from an adjacent bedroom closet boosted the privacy quotient of this bath designed to serve three growing boys.

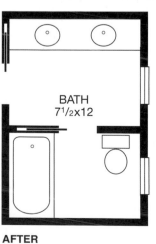

BATH
7¹/₂x12

4

AFTER

Bathtime for Kids

For a bunch of great ideas, browse the clever and fun kids' baths on these pages, and pick up some safety tips while you're at it.

Fast Lane and Accessible Too
Vintage signs, antique-car hubcaps, and wallpaper with mini automobiles drive this theme home.

The large working stoplight and the motor club sign balance the wallpaper's small scale. One-inch floor tiles provide good traction for a child rolling a wheelchair, and the sink offers plenty of roll-up room. Porcelain pieces beneath the sink prevent knees from bumping into hot and cold pipes.

And the Check Goes On
Checks and tiles go on and on in this lively bath (right). Countertops, walls, floor, and tub surround pink and yellow tiles mixed with green, cream, and some raspberry. Rope tiles frame windows, mirror, and decorative panels. On larger wall expanses the checkerboards turn on the diagonal or are arranged in quiltlike murals for variety.

Kid-Safe Bath Tips

Follow these tips to create a kid-safe bath environment.

- Choose cabinetry and countertops with rounded edges and corners.
- Use rugs with nonskid backings.
- Opt for skid-resistant flooring such as textured tile and vinyl.
- Install rubber footpads on step stools and chairs to prevent them from slipping.
- Store medicine outside the kids' bath in a childproof cabinet. Flush old medicine down the toilet.
- Equip electrical outlets with ground fault circuit interrupters.
- Arrange the bath so nothing can block the door. You need to be able to reach your child in an emergency.

Make Room for Baby

Topped with a thick, fabric-covered pad, a storage cabinet becomes a great spot for toweling off or changing a little one. The yellow and blue patterned wallpaper unifies the dark blue floor tiles and white cabinetry and counters. A blue plaid shower curtain makes a fresh, cottage-style statement. The Raggedy Ann lamp and framed storybook scenes are fanciful, charming touches.

Bandana Style

A white bath takes on a rough-and-tumble look with a few high-impact moves. Red bandana-style fabric makes a shower curtain and valance; crosshatched blue-over-white paint gives the walls a denim look. With bath mats and towels in bold blue and red, this formerly plain bath is as colorful as its users!

Water Smarts

Reduce mildew and water-related headaches with these moves.

- Keep a stack of absorbent towels near the tub for speedy puddle cleanups.
- Install a vent fan and keep it dust-free with an occasional swipe with a rag.
- Ask your paint supplier to mix a mildewcide into the paint you'll use.
- Choose easy-clean flooring such as tile, linoleum, or laminate rather than carpet.
- Lower your water-heater temperature to 120°F. As an added precaution install pressure-balanced faucets.
- Teach your children to sit in the bathtub and never to stand except to step out, slowly and safely.
- Drain the tub as soon as bathers are out.
- Install a childproof latch on the toilet lid.
- Lock other bathrooms to prevent little ones from venturing in.

Beach Feel

If your kids want privacy, and you want them to hustle through their morning routines, consider a floor plan like the one opposite. A door separates the toilet and tub/shower space from the double vanity area. Decked out in blue-sky beach colors, solid-surface counters with color-flecks, white cabinetry, white wall tile with blue accents, and matte-finish sandy hued floor tile, this bath is handsome and easily grows up with the kids' tastes. The family chose lever-style faucets for their ease of use and kid-friendly operation.

Rub-a-Ducky

Color-washed striped walls and stenciled accents make a cheery bath space for kids. A stencil that requires three colors was used to apply the ducks. Over a white cloud, the duck's yellow body gets an orange beak. The black outline is applied with a paint pen when the white, yellow, and orange is dry.

Kids Can Too

Encourage self-reliance and an I-can-do-it attitude. Consider these moves that will help your children do for themselves in the bath:

• Install door levers instead of knobs. They're easy to use, especially with wet hands.

• Mount towel bars and hooks low on the wall, where kids can hang their things themselves.

• Make step stools available, whether freestanding or the built-in, roll-out style.

• Provide open shelves to make tidying up easy.

• Consider handheld showerheads and pullout faucets; they're great for cleaning sinks and tubs as well as bodies.

Bold Blue

Two bedrooms with a bath between them is an ideal arrangement for siblings. Cobalt blue tile on counters and the tub surround is a bold and refreshing complement to white cabinetry. Accessories can change to accommodate evolving tastes as the kids grow—right now a sea theme works perfectly. Turtle-shape pulls on doors and drawers make it fun to put things away. Plentiful grout lines between the small floor tiles create a nonslip surface, which is a sound safety feature.

Color Sprite

Blocks of color and a multicolor band of tile around the floor energize this predominately white, gender-neutral bath. Set off with wallpaper that features paper dolls and dot patterns (on the ceiling) that appeal to kids, the tile scheme easily can accommodate a more adult look in the future. The hinged round mirror tilts for shorter and taller folks.

Primary Punch

Red laminate countertops, cobalt blue walls, and yellow and white floor tiles put the primary colors to good use in this functional bath for a pair of brothers. The white "guys only" shower curtain and personalized towels foster a sense of brotherhood, while the colorful fish wallpaper and a matching blind give the boys something fun to look at. The lantern sconces further the at-sea theme.

Storybook Sweet

A fanciful painted sink sets the tone for a multicolor, pattern-rich romantic bath. Yellow-and-white glazes turn existing wall tiles into a checkerboard. Metal primer and glazed polka dots give dash to an old radiator. The newly enameled tub is dressed with a mural and crowned with an old-style ceiling-mounted shower curtain ring.

Great bathrooms are those that have just the right mix of elements. This chapter explores fixtures, cabinetry, and lighting along with materials for countertops and flooring. Your options are vast—there are more products of more types and styles and with more features and functions than ever. If you've not been shopping for bath products lately, you'll find lots that are new. Some, such as synthetic stone countertops and laminate flooring, are reproductions of hard-to-find—and often hard-to-afford—premium natural materials. Others, such as linoleum, cork, or bamboo flooring, represent rediscovered or new earth-friendly products that also feature superior looks and performance. Use this chapter to prepare for what you'll find when you hit home centers and specialty shops in search of elements for your dream bath.

Style
Elements

Sinks and Faucets

From purely utilitarian to pointedly stylish, sinks come in multitudes of materials, types, and styles. Here's the lowdown:

Sink Materials

Porcelain-enamel cast-iron sinks are extremely durable and easy to care for, but are heavy and require sturdy support.

Vitreous china sinks have a lustrous, easy-clean surface and are available many choices of rich colors. They're lighter than porcelain-enamel cast-iron sinks and are the most resistant to discoloration and corrosion. Heavy items dropped in or on these sinks will crack or chip them.

Solid-surfacing material offers solid colors as well as stone look-alikes. One significant advantage: One-piece, integrated sinks and countertops are available in solid-surfacing for a seamless look and easy cleaning. Of these materials acrylic-resin is the most durable and requires little maintenance; polyester and cultured marble scratch and dull more readily.

Stainless-steel sinks are durable and unaffected by household chemicals; they do tend to show hard water and soap stains more readily than other materials.

Sink Styles

Pedestal sinks fit on top of a pedestal-shape base and are ideal for small baths. Their ledges offer little countertop surface and no base cabinet storage.

Wall-hung sinks wedge into small spaces and are a great choice for accessible baths, as you can install them at any height and they have a clear space underneath that allows for seated knee space and wheelchair access. These sinks share

the disadvantages of pedestal sinks, and the plumbing is not concealed.

Vanity sinks require the most floor space, but they have countertop space around them and cabinet storage below. Vanity sinks are available in several styles:

Self-rimming sinks are the most common and easiest to install. They have a rim that overlays the countertop and makes them easy to retrofit into existing countertops, as long as the opening is the same size. They also protect the particleboard substrate of laminate countertops from moisture damage. Debris can collect around the sink rim, but it's pretty simple to clean.

Undermount sinks mount to the bottom of a stone or solid-surfacing countertop, emphasizing the countertop material and making cleanup easy—debris sweeps directly from the counter into the sink without catching on a rim. Because undermount sinks expose the counter substrate, they require expert sink and countertop installation for a precise, clean fit.

Integrated bowl sinks are a sink and countertop combo—one seamless material used to form both. Material options are limited to stainless and solid-surfacing products and usually custom designs and special installations, which spikes the costs.

Vessel sinks appear to sit on top of the vanity counter like a bowl on a table. In reality most rest in a custom-cut hole in the vanity top.

Faucets

Years ago you could buy a faucet in any finish you liked—so long as it was polished chrome. That's still a favorite, but new coatings add a range of color to fixtures and make brass and gold hard-wearing enough to be practical.

Faucet Materials

Chrome finishes come polished, brushed, or matte. Polished chrome is extremely hard, easily cleaned, and doesn't oxidize; brushed or matte chrome has a softer appearance and is as durable as polished chrome. Inexpensive chrome sprayed over plastic parts tends to peel, so make sure the fixtures you buy are metal.

Brass fixtures are available in polished, satin, and antique finishes. Look for those with titanium finishes, which resist scratching, fading, and corrosion—problems common to standard brass finishes.

Baked enamel or epoxy coatings are available in many colors and are easy to clean. They're prone to chipping and fading over time, though, and some chemicals can damage their color.

Gold plate comes in polished, brushed, or matte finishes and has great visual appeal. Quality gold resists tarnish; matte finishes hide scratches. These fixtures are expensive, and quality can vary. The manufacturer must seal the finish or the gold remains vulnerable to damage.

Nickel is also available in polished, brushed, or matte finishes, and offers a softer tone than hard chrome. As with gold these fixtures are expensive, and quality varies depending on the manufacturer.

Faucet Types

Single-handle faucets have one spout and one handle that control the flow of both hot and cold water. They are generally safer and more convenient to use than their two-handled counterparts. With practice you can find the temperature you want on the first try. You also can turn the water on with your elbow or wrist when your hands are full or dirty.

Center-set faucets combine a spout and handle(s) in one unit. These faucets have either single-handle or double-handle controls. Most are designed for a three-hole basin, with the outside holes spaced 4 inches from center to center. However, some have a single-post design that requires only one hole.

Spread-fit faucets separate spout and handles. The connection between them is concealed below the sink deck. Installers can adapt them to fit holes spaced from 4 to 10 inches apart. You can individualize them even more if they are mounted on a countertop next to the sink. For example you can place the spout on a rear corner and the handles off to one side. These faucets are handy for tight installations that lack the room for a full faucet at the back of the sink basin. They also are ideal for whirlpool tubs, so that the handles are accessible from outside the tub for filling. This type of faucet offers a more traditional look than single-handle faucets, and you can combine different style handles and spouts for a custom look.

Wall-mount faucets are attached to the wall as opposed to the sink or the counter. These faucets are designed for unusually shaped sinks, such as antique bowls or other vessels that have been modified for use in the bath.

1 The front of a china bowl sink extends past the edge of its supporting countertop for a gracious, supported look.
2 Skirts can dress a pedestal sink and hide toiletries and supplies beneath.

Bathtubs

Tubs range in type and style from the familiar to the exotic. Whether you're buying a conventional tub, a whirlpool, or a soaking tub, here's what to look for.

Materials

Both whirlpools and standard tubs come in the following materials:

Enameled cast-iron tubs are made from iron cast into a bathtub-shape mold and finished with enamel. They are thicker than other tubs and retain heat very well when filled with hot water. Durable and solid, these tubs also come in a variety of color options. Cast-iron tubs are heavy, so you may need to reinforce your bathroom floor and come up with a plan for getting one into your bathroom.

Enameled steel tubs have the same glassy, scratch-resistant surface as their heavier cast-iron counterparts, but they're less expensive. They also come in fewer color options, they're noisy when being filled with water, are more prone to chipping, and feel less solid. They lose heat rapidly.

Fiberglass backing material is finished with a smooth layer of polyester to create tubs. Wood or metal reinforcement makes the tub feel solid. These inexpensive units are available in a wide choice of styles and shapes, and they're lightweight, making them easier to install. Unfortunately the polyester finish is not as durable as either enamel or acrylic, and the tubs fail to retain heat well.

Acrylic tubs, made of acrylic sheets that are heated and formed in a mold, are reinforced with fiberglass and wood or metal backing. These tubs are available in a wide choice of styles and shapes, and are lightweight. More expensive than fiberglass tubs, acrylic tubs hold heat better (if properly insulated), but the finish is prone to scratches.

Cast-polymer tubs are made of solid-color, polymer-based materials often patterned to resemble a natural stone such as granite or marble. Thicker than acrylic and covered in polyester gel, the tubs hold heat well but are not as durable as either acrylic or enameled cast-iron tubs.

1 *The faucet's center, wall-mounted position makes this tub a good soaker for two and doesn't hinder stepping in.*
2 *Mounted on the corner, leading edge of this tub, this faucet makes it easy to control water temperature and won't get in the way.*

1

Water Ways

Spout Spots:

Where you place a tub spout and faucet handles may seem to be a matter of personal preference, but access, safety, and maintenance are issues to consider. Though built-in tub/shower enclosures typically feature the spout and controls mounted together on the wall at one end, whirlpools and deck-mounted tubs allow other positions. Determine during the design stage of your project where you want the spout .

The Soaking Tub Alternative:

If you haven't shopped for bath appliances in quite some time, you'll be surprised to encounter soaking tubs. They're gaining favor with those whose idea of indulgence is a deep, still soak in warm water rather than the motion and pressure that's part of the jetted tub experience. Of course you can soak in a standard tub, but it's much more luxurious to do so in a deep, up-to-your-neck vessel that measures 20 to 22 inches or more in height.

Getting in Hot Water:

The National Kitchen and Bath Association recommends that your hot water heater be at least two-thirds the capacity of your tub: A 60-gallon hot water tank will serve a 90-gallon tub adequately, but the rest of the water in your house will be cold after the tub is filled. Your new tub manual tells you how many gallons of water it takes to fill the tub.

If your hot water heater is too small for the big whirlpool or soaking tub you're thinking of installing, you can either install a bigger heater or install two heaters side by side. You can also buy a whirlpool tub with an in-line heater of its own. Instead of heating water before use like a hot water tank heater, an in-line heater maintains the temperature of the water in the tub for the duration of your bath. If you plan to soak for long periods, an in-line heater is a good idea regardless of the capacity of your hot water heater.

3

Styles

Recessed tubs have one finished side, called an apron, and three unfinished sides that fit against two end walls and a back wall. Models are available with a drain at either end to fit your plumbing needs. People with limited mobility may find it difficult to get in and out of these tubs.

Corner tubs fit diagonally between two corners, taking up less space than other tubs. Like standard recessed tubs, most have only one finished side. Some models, however, have a finished side and end.

Freestanding tubs are finished on all four sides, and you can place them almost anywhere in a room. Old-fashioned freestanding claw-foot tubs are available and look great in traditional baths. You can also find freestanding models that have a contemporary look.

Platform tubs don't have unfinished panels because they are dropped into raised platforms. Depending on the platform design, you can place them anywhere: against a wall, in a corner, even in the center of a room.

Showers and Showerheads

3

Three basic types of shower stalls dominate this category.

Prefabricated stalls are available in many shapes and colors. These stalls are available in one-piece, two-piece, or three-piece versions. The most common material for these units is fiberglass with a finish surface of acrylic or other plastic. Tempered glass combined with fiberglass stalls is also available. Sizes range from 32 inches square (too small to meet some local codes) to 36×48 inches. One-piece versions are typically reserved for new construction (including new additions) because like tubs and whirlpools, one-piece stalls are very large and can be difficult to get through doorways. Two- and three-piece models readily fit through most door openings. Shower doors or curtains are typically sold separately. Some stalls come with their own pan, or flooring piece, while others require a separate pan. Prefabricated stalls are available in three shapes: square, rectangular, and neo-angle—which has two sides, a diagonal front and are designed to fit against a wall or into a corner. The walls of the stall are attached to standard wall framing for support.

Prefabricated shower pans are molded floor pieces that are available in various materials, such as plastic and stone. You can combine them with prefabricated shower stalls or custom-made solid-surfacing or tile walls.

Custom-made stalls offer the most design flexibility; they're made to suit your needs and desires. Any waterproof material can be used for the walls, including tile, marble, solid-surfacing, tempered glass, or glass block.

Showerheads

These days you can choose the standard showerhead or surround yourself with mists and sprays galore. Here are some of the types of shower heads available:

Wall-mount showerheads are affordable. The showerhead adjusts via a ball joint where it joins the neck. Models that offer varying spray types fit the needs of most users.

Ceiling-mount showerheads work well in areas where the ceiling is too low to accommodate a wall-mount head. Some are also quite large and produce a waterfall-like feel. Because the spray comes from overhead, it is difficult to avoid getting your hair wet when washing in this type of shower.

Handheld showerheads clip on to a 3- to 6-foot-long hose that lets you spray the water where you want it. It's a versatile choice that makes it easy to wash your hair, rinse off, or scrub down the shower itself.

Sliding bar showerheads slide up and down on a bar mounted on the wall. Because the spray height is extremely easy to adjust, it's a good option when the users vary in height.

Body spray and body mist shower sprays are installed in vertical rows on opposite or adjacent walls, creating a crisscross water massage between knee and shoulder levels that lets you wash up quickly without getting your hair wet.

Body spa shower panels are installed against one or more walls of the shower stall. The panels are equipped with water jets arranged vertically from knee to neck level. Similar to the jets in a whirlpool tub, the water jets pump out and circulate large quantities of water for a powerful massage.

Steam It Up

Equip your shower stalls with a top and a door that seals tightly, and your shower becomes an opulent steam bath. To do this you'll need to install a vapor barrier on the ceiling and wall framing to keep the moisture from reaching the studs and joists and thereby causing rot. You'll also have to install a steam generator somewhere outside the shower.

1 *Despite all the choices in showerheads, standard models with spray variations still work well. Here one is mounted over an oval, diagonally placed tub.*

2 *Broad, circular rainfall-style showerheads make a terrific shower experience. If you like to shower occasionally without getting your hair wet, make sure you have an alternate spray source, though.*

Toilets, Bidets, and Lighting

Toilets

You have a choice of classic two-piece toilets or low-profile, single-piece units. Models with elongated bowls are more comfortable and more expensive than standard round toilets. By law all toilets manufactured after January 1, 1994, must use no more than 1.6 gallons of water per flush. Whatever style you choose you have the option of three types of "low flow" flushing mechanisms.

Gravity-flush toilets are the least expensive option. These toilets work using the same principles as models produced before the low-flow mandate. The weight of the water flowing down from the tank clears the bowl. The water pressure in your neighborhood affects how well your gravity-assisted toilets work. Most manufacturers recommend about 25 pounds of pressure per square inch to work best. (Your water pressure can also fluctuate with household activities such as turning on the lawn sprinklers.) Though relatively easy to install, these models don't discharge waste as effectively as the following options.

Pressure-assisted toilets use pressurized air from a vessel hidden in the toilet tank to force water into the bowl and down the drain. The most effective low-flow option, these toilets are noisier than the gravity flush and are more expensive to repair. They can also cost three to six times more than base-model gravity-flush toilets.

Pump-assisted toilets eliminate waste with an electric pump that propels water into the bowl and down the drain. Sold for about five times the cost of a base-model gravity-flush toilet, these work nearly as well as pressure-assisted toilets but are quieter.

If you want to keep your current high-flow toilet but would like to reduce its water consumption, you can displace some of the water in the tank by placing a water-filled plastic bottle there. Or you can install a dual flusher that allows a half-flush for liquid-only waste.

The Bidet

Although not used as widely in the United States as they are in Europe, bidets are gaining in popularity. The fixture resembles a toilet but actually works more like a sink. Water ascends from the center of the bowl to rinse the posterior of the person sitting on the bowl. Both genders can safely use a bidet.

Unlike a toilet, a bidet must be plumbed with both hot and cold

1

Easy Cleaning

Unbroken lines make one-piece toilets easier to clean than two-piece models. Wide bowls require less scrubbing than narrow ones because the wider design does a better job of clearing waste. Toilets with straight sides that hide the bolts that secure it to the floor are also easier to wipe clean than models with lots of lumps and bumps.

water, as well as a drain. For convenience locate the bidet close to the toilet. If the two fixtures are installed side by side, leave at least 15 inches between them. Expect the fixture to take up at least 3 square feet of floor space.

Lighting

You'll likely need a combination of fixtures to fully light your bath.

Recessed downlights, also called can lights, are the least obtrusive fixture for general or task lighting. Position them close enough together so that their light patterns can overlap.

Pendent lights hung from a wire or chain are suited to both overall ambient light and task lighting over the vanity.

Surface-mount fixtures work well in bathrooms that can't accommodate recessed fixtures—a common problem in bath remodeling.

Wall sconces placed on both sides of a mirror offer shadow-free task light for applying makeup or shaving. Select bulbs designed for vanity illumination: These produce a daylight spectrum that gives you a better idea of how you'll look outside the bathroom than ordinary incandescent or fluorescent bulbs do.

Shower-safe fixtures are water- and steam-proof. Most building codes require that only shower-safe lights can be installed in shower stalls. One centrally located fixture installed on the ceiling or high on the wall usually is enough to adequately light a shower stall. In a tub area place the fixture so that it doesn't shine directly in your eyes as you recline in the tub.

Night-lights make late-night or early morning trips to the bathroom safer and more comfortable for people of all ages. For an easy, affordable solution, plug in an automatic night-light that turns on by itself when the room darkens. Or install a low-voltage system below the vanity toe-kick or around shelving to provide soft nighttime illumination.

1 *Sconce lighting is an elegant choice in the bath. These are mounted on either side of the mirror and feature milky glass shades. Sconce lights can be mounted directly into mirrors as well*

2 *At this double vanity, pairs of slim halogen pendants loop over each mirror for a bright, modern look. Halogen lights are especially nice on dimmer switches.*

Countertops

Countertops are available in various styles and materials—each with its own properties. Look for something that will stand up to water, soap, alcohol- and acetone-based liquids, as well as toothpaste and cosmetics.

Stone

Granite is prized for its natural beauty and durability, whether it is polished to a high gloss or honed to a pleasing matte finish. Its sparkly, variegated, crystalline structure makes for a lively play of light on its surface. Solid granite is expensive; for a lower-cost option, consider 12×12-inch granite tiles.

Marble is much softer and more porous than granite. It sometimes fractures along veining and offers less resistance to stains, scratches, and general wear. To ensure a longer life, seal marble regularly. Costs for both solid pieces and tiles are similar to granite.

Limestone is more porous than marble. Ranging from light beige to golden brown in color, it is typically given a honed finish. Seal limestone properly and keep acidic substances away from it.

Slate is dense and nonabsorbent, and known for its blue-gray color, though it comes in other shades. Because of its low absorption rate and density, slate is highly resistant to stains, bacteria, and heat. Clean with water and a mild soap, and buff out scratches.

1

Soapstone has a gray to green color and a silky, soapy feel. It may be familiar—for years it has been used as a work surface in laboratories and science classrooms. Soapstone is highly resistant to acids and water. Seal with mineral oil and regularly re-oil it to maintain a uniform dark color. Remove any scratches with sandpaper and water.

Stone Stand-Ins

The same elements that make stone beautiful—its natural colors, the variegations in pattern, and its porous structure—create challenges when it comes to using the material in a bath. To counteract these natural limitations, stone-base products offer many desirable color options and eliminate some maintenance issues.

Engineered quartz, which is made from quartz bound together with space-age polymers, has an appearance, composition, weight, and price that is comparable to granite. Its surface captures the crystalline sparkle and density

of granite but is nonporous so it requires no sealing and is less susceptible to stains. Manufacturers claim that it's tougher than granite and less susceptible to chipping and cracking.

Enameled lavastone is natural stone that has been glazed with high-temperature enamel. The high heat results in a durable surface with vivid colors and a glasslike sheen. The visible pores of the lavastone and the thin cracks—or crazing—of the enamel create a one-of-a-kind product. The nonporous surface is resistant to water, oils, acids, and other substances. It will scratch, so cleaning with nonabrasive detergents and water is recommended.

Laminated stone is made of thin sheets of granite or marble backed by fiberglass and is lighter in weight and more flexible than solid stone. The 5×10-foot sheets, which start at a thickness of 2¼ inches, are appropriate for walls, floors and countertops).

1 *Slipped into this vanity niche, a small piece of granite countertop material fits within a budget plan. A stainless-steel sink mounts beneath it.*

2 *Plain white tile counters are dressed to delight a youngster with baseball-themed trim tiles around the backsplash.*

Solid-surfacing, made entirely of plastic resin composites, comes in a variety of thicknesses and colors, patterns, and natural-material look-alikes. The nonporous material is known for its design flexibility, which allows for the creation of special effects using inlays of contrasting colors. Color runs through the material, so nicks aren't so noticeable. Solid-surfacing resists stains, but is susceptible to scratches and scorches. Minor damage, however, can be sanded out. Costs are similar to granite.

Other materials

Concrete is an increasingly popular countertop option. It comes in the standard gray, or it may be dyed and inlaid with other elements to create custom looks. The material must be sealed regularly but it is still subject to stains. Some concrete counters feature inlaid materials, such as metal or stone, for a decorative look. Others have metal forms that remain in place, adding a contrasting gleam to the edge of the grainy material. Cost is somewhat less than stone.

Ceramic tile comes in a host of colors, patterns, and textures. Its decorative possibilities—borders, geometric designs, or mosaics—are endless. It is moisture resistant; the tiles themselves wipe clean with a damp cloth, but the grout joints can stain. To minimize discoloration, install a tiled countertop using narrow grout joints, epoxy grout, and a darker color grout. Costs vary widely with the complexity of the pattern and the price of the tiles themselves.

Glass slabs create a dramatic effect in guest baths or other rooms that are not used daily. Frosted glass hides scratches and water spots better than clear glass.

Laminate is an affordable, durable, low-maintenance surface that offers a tremendous range of colors, patterns, textures, and look-alikes. Prolonged exposure to water in some cases dissolves glue lines and causes the subsurface to warp. Better grades of laminate feature color through the material, making scratches and chips less visible. Laminate countertop sections are available in a variety of front edge treatments, with or without attached backsplashes. Laminate is one of the least expensive of all the countertop options.

Stone Care

Stone surfaces are durable, but not impervious to everything. To prevent stains from oils, acids, and water deposits, apply a sheen-free penetrating sealer at installation and as recommended by the manufacturer thereafter. Typically, polished-granite countertops require a sealer once every two years.

For very porous limestone and marble, annual application of a surface sealer creates a barrier against water and stains. But surface sealers can scratch and may build up and dull the look of the stone.

To keep slate looking rich, many homeowners rub in mineral oil weekly or monthly. It blends out the marks and gives the slate a dark look. Or, every three to five years use an "ager" that seals the stone and enhances its color.

Flooring

Choose a flooring based on a balance of comfort, good looks, maintenance, and durability.

Stone is an elegant choice. Harder varieties, notably granite, require little maintenance and are nearly indestructible. Others, such as more porous marble and limestone, stain easily and require more care and maintenance. Some, like slate, are prone to cracking and chipping. Like ceramic tile, stone can be cold, hard, and unforgiving. It tends to be expensive; professional installation is often required.

Ceramic tile comes in a variety of sizes and colors that allow you to create exciting patterns. You'll find tiles glazed and unglazed. A glazed finish is a good choice for bathrooms because it prevents moisture from soaking in. Glazed tiles eventually show some wear in high-traffic areas. Ceramic tile is durable, generally low maintenance, and moisture resistant. On the downside it can feel cold and dirt often collects in the grout lines. Cost for both the materials and installation varies widely, depending on the tile type and dimensions, complexity of the design, and the amount of subfloor preparation required.

Bamboo is an option that's becoming an increasingly popular choice for its appearance, durability, and eco-friendly nature. It looks a lot like hardwood, but it's actually three layers of grass that have been laminated under high pressure to create planks. Three coats of acrylic urethane make the surface durable and resistant to water, mildew, and insect damage. Harder than maple and oak, bamboo also expands and contracts less. Bamboo flooring comes unfinished or prefinished and is glued or nailed to the subfloor. Cost is fairly high.

Cork provides a resilient, cushioned surface underfoot that is noiseless, comfortable, and moisture-resistant. Made from renewable bark harvested from cork oak trees in Mediterranean forests, cork requires a urethane finish to assure easy sweeping and mopping. If the old finish is sanded every few years and new urethane is applied, cork flooring can last for decades. It comes in tiles or planks that allow for easy repair should the floor be damaged; installation is similar to vinyl tile. Cost is on the higher end of moderate.

Laminate offers the look of wood, tile, stone, and other natural materials at a lower price. Earlier laminate required installers to glue planks together—a tedious process that sometimes resulted in failed joints and moisture damage. New laminates snap together, cutting the installation time significantly. According to the manufacturers, new laminate has tighter, more even, watertight joints. However, some laminate products are not recommended for use in bathrooms; in fact, most manufacturers recommend mopping up standing water promptly. Laminate is available in squares, strips, or rectangles. It is durable, easy to clean, and requires little or no maintenance. Keep in mind that you can't refinish or restain laminate like wood. Costs are moderate.

Linoleum, which is made of primarily natural materials, is making a comeback. Often confused with vinyl, which is made from petroleum-based polyvinyl chloride, linoleum is made of natural linseed oil, resin, cork, limestone, and wood flour mixed with pigments, then rolled onto a jute backing and dried. Soft underfoot, it comes in both tiles and sheets of solid or flecked colors, and is easy to care for. As the linseed oil dries, it actually becomes harder and more durable than vinyl.

Although old-style linoleum tended to fade over time, today's version offers bright, lasting color. Cost is on the higher end of moderate.

Hardwood brings warmth and a classic look into the bath. It is available in many species—prefinished or unfinished—in solid, engineered, or parquet form. Solid planks are most common. You can sand and refinish them many times if they become stained or damaged, giving them a long life. Engineered planks consist of two or more layers of wood laminated together—a hardwood veneer wear layer and lower layers of softwood. Because the wear layer is relatively thin, you can only refinish an engineered wood floor a limited number of times. Generally, solid wood floors are site-finished while engineered wood floors are prefinished. In both cases new clear finishes are tougher, more durable, and more water resistant than ever. Wood is still susceptible to water damage in high-traffic areas. Cost is moderate.

Vinyl is a good-looking, low-cost, easy-care choice. You'll find an enormous selection of colors and styles, including well-designed stone, tile, and hardwood look-alikes. Available as sheet goods and tiles (including easy-to-install, self-stick tiles), vinyl in tile form eventually loosens, admitting moisture and dirt. Less expensive vinyl grades can puncture, fade, and discolor quickly, but good-quality sheet vinyl is easy to maintain and can last for many years. Cost is low, although do-it-yourselfers may find that they can install laminate, tile, or wood for little, if any, increase in cost.

1 *Small tiles and the grout that sets them make an easy-clean, nonslip surface—ideal for bathrooms and shower stalls. The choices are endless, ranging from solid colors to translucent colored glass, flecked ceramic, and mixed tones. Mix and match them to create myriad patterns and borders.*

Glass in the Bath

Until recently the use of glass in the bath was limited to mirrors, standard see-through windows, and perhaps a shelf or two. Lately, however, manufacturers have embraced the magic of glass, using the material in many forms, textures, and colors in myriad products. Now you can bring sparkle, light, and see-through illusion to nearly every bathroom surface.

Day or night, glass plays with light to create lively, enchanting spaces. Your eye doesn't stop when it encounters glass. The transparent quality yields an expansive illusion, even if there's nothing beyond but drywall. The baths shown on these pages reveal ways to bring glass magic into your bath no matter what the scope of your project is.

1 *You can use textured glass as cabinet and door inserts. Use it for dividers that*

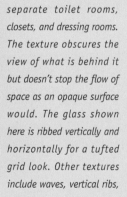

separate toilet rooms, closets, and dressing rooms. The texture obscures the view of what is behind it but doesn't stop the flow of space as an opaque surface would. The glass shown here is ribbed vertically and horizontally for a tufted grid look. Other textures include waves, vertical ribs, and pebbles.

2 *A contemporary stainless-steel and translucent glass pedestal sink grabs your attention in this simple bath. A half-wall of translucent sea-blue glass tiles is both practical and aesthetically pleasing.*

3 *In this small, space-smart bath, a glassblock window pulls in light from an interior space. A standard mirror would normally occupy this window location. Instead an adjustable mirror mounted on the wall swings in.*

4 *A full powder-room wall of ribbed glass blocks draws in waves of diffused light, forming a sparkling, geometric backdrop for this contemporary vanity and mirror arrangement. The stainless-steel-framed mirror hangs from the ceiling. Plate glass forms the vanity countertop that sits on a rectangular stainless frame. You can use glass block walls on interior or exterior walls and in contemporary as well as traditional settings.*

4

Now that you know how to make a bath more efficient and beautiful, this chapter offers additional insights to help launch your dream.

First a review of the elements of good bath design provides information for building a bath that has the right amount of room in the right places. You'll also find a two-page section on barrier-free baths.

The bath design kit allows you to play with different ideas, room shapes, fixture placements, and configurations on paper. Some advice on how to hire the best design and contracting professionals you can find and how to determine the building codes in your community follows.

Before you actually begin work on your bath, you'll want to know how to break your project into steps and phases so the process is easier to manage. You'll find tips on how to make changes and additions appear seamless and how to make sure your bath is well-integrated with the rooms around it, whether they're guest bedrooms or rooms that make up a master suite.

Finally check out the tips for surviving a bath construction or remodeling project, so you can enjoy the process as well as the result.

Use these strategies to help you begin your bathroom adventure on the right foot—and keep it on track all the way to completion.

Strategies &
Insights

Designing Your Bath

When you're ready to put the whole package together, it's time to design the room. Read through these options for getting the job done and choose the best one for you.

Design it yourself. Guided by recommended minimum clearances on page 178-179, and aided by our bathroom designing kit on pages 182-184, sketch your space, mark the location of existing features, and try different options on for size. You may well want or need to consult a professional, but the exercise of working through a variety of options yourself will help clarify your priorities before you talk to a designer, architect, or licensed contractor.

Get home center design help. Many home center stores have staff who can help you lay out a bath at little or no charge. If you want stock cabinets and fixtures, these folks can be a terrific help, streamlining the design and product selection process. The level of help provided and the designer talent vary widely, so before you decide to go this route, check out their qualifications and client satisfaction as carefully you would any other design specialists. Bring accurate measurements and be aware that you probably won't get much customizing or problem-solving help.

Hire a design specialist. Bathrooms can be such complex rooms that it is helpful to have a professional bath designer on your team. These pros combine knowledge of interior design with an emphasis on bath function. They're also up-to-date on new bath products and the latest technology. Certified designers have completed a course of study designed by the National Kitchen and Bath Association. You'll find plenty of talent among both certified and noncertified designers.

Consult an interior designer. Most interior designers address bathrooms as well as other rooms in the house. If you're remodeling more than a bath—for instance, if you're adding a master suite—you might chose an interior designer to assist you with the entire project.

Commission an architect. Architects are especially valuable when significant structural changes

1

1 *In this top-floor master bath, good design was essential to making all the elements fit within a confined space. A winglike countertop draws the eye across the room, and transoms along the top of the walls enhance the distribution of light into this private area.*

to your home are in order, such as building a master suite addition or reworking your home's internal structure.

Seamless Additions

If your bathroom remodeling involves an addition, blend it seamlessly with the rest of the home. Details make a major difference, so pay attention to three crucial factors: roofline, proportion, and materials.

• **Start at the top.** Make sure all roof portions mirror one another in style. Match the pitch, overhangs, soffits, fasciae, and eaves with the existing structure.

• **Maintain proportion.** Take care that your addition won't overwhelm, or be overwhelmed by, the existing structure.

• **Choose materials carefully.** On the roof, match shingle style, color, and material; when using brick, match its color, size, texture, and mortar to the original. Or complement the existing materials with something consistent with the period of the house. Windows, too, need to match, both in basic type and the details, such as muntin width and pane size. Last, paint both the new and existing structures in colors that are appropriate for the style and the period of your home, and choose a color palette that is in keeping with its surroundings.

Visualizing Your New Bath

Once you have a preliminary design, use these tips to visualize the new space and make it work for you.

Chalk it out. If you're working on a major addition, outline its shape using stakes and string in the area where you're planning to build it. To get some sense of a bath that uses existing space within the house, use children's driveway chalk to outline a life-size rendition of the room on your driveway, cement garage or

2

basement floor—anywhere you have sufficient room. Mark the locations of walls, doors, windows, fixtures, cabinets, and amenities. Walk around the "space" and see how it feels. Imagine what it would be like to use the room on a daily basis.

Ask for a rendering. Your architect or designer can provide you with three-dimensional color drawings, complete with fixtures, architectural features, and lighting sketched in. Renderings give you a much better feel for the prospective space than blueprints do.

Take a virtual tour. Your design professional also might offer to let you "tour" your project before it's constructed using a computer-aided

2 *Thick-tiled walls form the toilet compartment and shape the shower space in this bath. A wall-mounted sheet of glass keeps water from escaping the shower without the user feeling closed in; a rainfall-style showerhead delivers a quick, satisfying soaking.*

design (CAD) program. This software lets you experiment with configurations and view the space in three dimensions from different vantage points.

After you study the floor plan or model in conjunction with how you live, make adjustments as necessary to create a bath tailored to fit.

Elements of Good Design

Remodeling success is measured in comfort, function, and personal style. Ergonomics—the characteristics of the human body that you must consider when arranging the fixtures—play a significant role in bath design. So does safety, and your home's plumbing layouts. You'll also need to plan for proper lighting, ventilation, conservative water usage, and noise reduction.

Minimum Clearances

Based on needs and average human measurements, the National Kitchen and Bath Association (NKBA) has created bath design guidelines that specify the minimum space needed for various bath components. These guidelines work well for people at all life stages, although some of the dimensions will need to be adjusted for a completely barrier-free bath (see pages 180 and 181). Keep in mind that these are recommended minimums, not hard-and-fast rules. Allow more space if the fit is tight for the intended users.

Floor Space Guidelines

The amount of clear floor space required at each fixture may overlap. That is, you can add together the clear space between a toilet and a tub—just make sure the amount of space between the two meets the minimum guidelines for both.

Door openings. Make all doorways at least 32 inches wide. Allow a clear floor space at least the width of the door on the push side and a larger clear floor space on the pull side to allow the users enough room to open, close, and pass through the doorway comfortably.

Walkways. Make passages between the walls and fixtures at least 36 inches wide.

Sink fronts. Leave at least 30×48 inches (parallel or perpendicular) of clear floor space in front of each sink. If there is open knee space under the sink, up to 12 of the 48 inches can extend beneath the sink.

Toilet allowance. Leave a clear floor space of 48×48 inches in front of the toilet. If floor area is limited, a 30×48-inch space may be adequate. Leave at least 16 inches of space from the centerline of the fixture to the closest fixture or sidewall. Allow at least 1 inch between the back of the water tank and the wall behind it. If you plan to install a toilet in a separate compartment, make the compartment at least 36 inches wide and 66 inches long. Install a swing-out door or a pocket door on the opening to the compartment. Make the doorway at least 32 inches wide.

Bidet allowance. Leave a clear floor space of 48×48 inches in front of the bidet. Leave at least 16 inches of space from the fixture's centerline to the closest fixture or sidewall. When the toilet and bidet are adjacent, maintain a minimum of 16 inches clearance to all obstructions.

Bathtub clearance. Plan for at least a 30×60-inch section of clear space adjacent to the tub if you plan to approach the fixture from the side. Leave 48×60 inches of clear floor space if you'll be approaching it from the front.

Shower entrance. For showers less than 60 inches wide, plan a clear floor space that is 36 inches deep and 12 inches wider than the shower. For wider showers plan for a clear floor space that is 36 inches deep and as wide as the shower.

Shower interior. The minimum

useable interior dimensions—measured from wall to wall—are 34×34 inches, but most people prefer more space. If you're faced with little space, you can reduce this to 32×32 inches, but doing so might make the shower uncomfortable for some users. Design the shower doors so they open into the bathroom—not into the stall.

Grooming Space Guidelines

These NKBA guidelines ensure that everyone in the bath has adequate grooming space and elbowroom near the sink, vanities, and countertops.

Sink space. Leave a clearance of at least 15 inches from the centerline of the sink to the closest sidewall. If the vanity has two sinks, leave at least 30 inches of clearance between the centerlines of each. If the sinks are wider than 30 inches,

increase the distance by several inches to provide a minimum of 8 inches of open counter space between the sinks. This space allows ample elbowroom when both sinks are in use.

Vanity height. If you are including two vanities, make them different heights—one between 30 and 34 inches high and one between 34 and 42 inches high—or match the comfort level of the people who use them. Vanity cabinets are typically 29 to 30 inches high, while kitchen base cabinets are typically 36 inches high. Many people find the 36-inch height more comfortable for standing. If space allows add a 30-inch-high section with knee space below for comfortable sitting.

Mirror height. When locating a mirror above a vanity, make sure that its bottom edge is no more than

40 inches above the floor. If the top of the mirror is tilted away from the wall, its bottom edge can be as much as 48 inches above the floor.

Door and drawer widths. When designing a vanity cabinet, split cabinet doors that are 24 inches or wider. Large single doors can be awkward to open, especially in a narrow bathroom. Avoid narrow doors and drawers. Nine-inch widths are too narrow to be useful.

Corner comfort. To eliminate sharp corners, only use countertops with rounded corners.

1 *Good bathroom design includes enough floor space to enjoy all the amenities. Plan at least a 30×60-inch section of clear floor adjacent to the tub if, or in this bath, you approach it from the side.*

Barrier-Free Baths

The goal of a barrier-free bath is to allow all users to be as independent and comfortable as possible. Even if no one in your home has special needs now, planning a bath that can accommodate wheelchairs and walkers can make guests—or even a kid with a cast—feel welcome and more comfortable. Take a look at "Universal Design to Grow On" on pages 106-109.

Location, location, location. Creating a barrier-free bath starts with the room's location. It must be situated on the home's ground floor so that there are no stairs to climb up or down.

Door size. Thirty-four-inch door openings are ideal. Larger openings are difficult to open and close from a seated position. Narrow openings are difficult, if not impossible, for a wheelchair to get through.

Handle selection. Equip entrance doors, showers, and faucets with lever or D-shape handles. They are easier to operate than knobs, especially for young children and people with arthritis or limited mobility.

Floor space. For a typical-size wheelchair to make a complete turnaround, you'll need a circular area of clear floor space measuring 5 feet in diameter. Leave an area in front of the sink that measures at least 30×48 inches (although the clear floor space can overlap). Toilets need a clear floor space 48 inches square. Bathtubs need a clear floor space of 60×60 inches.

Shower stalls. Shower stalls are easier to get in and out of than tubs. Choose a stall with no curb or a very short one. Slope the floor toward the drain to ensure that the water stays within the enclosure. Make shower stalls at least 4 feet square with openings at least 36 inches wide. Include a seat that is 17 to 19 inches above the floor, grab bars, a single-handle lever control, and a handheld shower spray.

1 *A simple ramp makes the entrance to this accessible shower easier than trying to drive over the threshold. Clear space in front of the tub enables a wheelchair user to transfer from chair to tub and back again. The front-mount tub faucets present easy accessibility from both inside and outside the tub.*

2 *This traditional-style bath provides for roll-up grooming. Narrow drawers on both sides of the sink keep toothbrushes and other toiletries handy. A ruglike pattern in the nonslip blue and white tile flooring adds warmth without inhibiting wheelchair maneuverability.*

Bathtubs. If a tub is necessary, install grab bars in the tub along the sidewall and the two end walls. Install the bars 33 to 36 inches above the tub bottom and another set 9 inches above the tub rim. All bars should be at least 24 inches long.

Knee space. Make the knee space under a sink about 27 inches high and 30 inches wide. In addition

insulate or conceal hot water pipes to protect users from scalding.

Toilet tank. The ideal placement for a toilet is in a corner of the bath where you can install grab bars both behind the toilet and next to it. Leave at least 48 inches of clear floor space to either one side or in front of the toilet. A toilet 3 inches higher than a conventional model makes it much easier to transfer to or from a wheelchair. Generally grab bars are 33 to 36 inches above the floor and measure 42 inches long on a sidewall and not more than 12 inches from the back wall. The bar on the back wall should be at least 24 inches long and extend at least 12 inches from each side of the center of the toilet.

Grab bars. Rated to withstand up to 300 pounds of pressure, grab bars are efficient only if they are attached securely. Secure grab bars to wall studs, or if possible, before

putting up drywall, install ¾-inch plywood sheathing over the studs from floor to ceiling. You can then install bars anywhere on the walls as needed. Buy bars with a nonslip texture. They come in a variety of colors and styles to blend with most any bath décor.

Windows. Casement windows are the easiest type window for anyone in a wheelchair to open. Install windows 24 to 30 inches above the floor so that wheelchair users can open, close, and easily see out of them.

Barrier-Free Information
Barrier-Free Environments, P.O. Box 30634, Raleigh, NC 27633; 919/782-7823
Abledata, 8630 Fenton St., Suite 930, Silver Spring, MD 20910; 800/227-0216; www.abledata.com

For Safety's Sake

• **Grab bars.** Reinforce walls for grab bars at the time of construction. Install grab bars in the tub, shower, and toilet areas.
• **GFCI outlets.** Protect all receptacles, lights, and switches in the room with ground fault circuit interrupters (GFCI), which reduce the risk of electrical shocks. Install only moistureproof light fixtures above the tub and shower areas.
• **Shower and tub surround safety.** Include a bench or seat that is 17 to 19 inches above the floor and at least 15 inches deep. It can be a hanging or folding seat; to support the seat, you will need to reinforce the wall when you install the surround. To reduce the risk of falls, avoid installing steps for climbing into the shower or tub. Design the surround so you can reach the controls from inside and outside the stall. Put the controls 38 to 48 inches above the floor and above the grab bar if there is one. Locate the controls between the showerhead and the stall door. For a handheld showerhead, locate the head no higher than 48 inches above the floor in its lowest position. To help prevent cuts and bruises, add a cushion to the tub spout. (Waterproof cushions in various shapes are readily available at bath and hardware centers.) Install only laminated safety glass with a plastic inner layer, tempered glass, or approved plastic for any clear face of a shower or tub enclosure or partition that reaches to within 18 inches of the floor.
• **Water safety.** Set the hot water heater to 120 degrees F to prevent scalding. Or install a pressure-balancing temperature regulator or a temperature-limiting device for all faucet heads, particularly showerheads.

Bath Design Kit

Few homeowners resist the urge to sketch out some ideas, even if they plan to work with a designer or architect. Go ahead! Your drawings will provide better insight into what you're after. Use the Bath Design Kit on the following pages to work through the process.

To help you consider how you'll use your new bath, visualize how the rooms' various zones—washing, bathing, toilet, storage, and perhaps sitting, exercising, or even snacking—relate to one another. Figure out where you'd like these various zones to go and how the bath relates to the surrounding rooms such as bedrooms, walk-in closets, dressing rooms, halls, or sitting rooms. Finally, consider what architectural features you'd like to add or highlight and what types, sizes, and styles of fixtures, cabinetry, shelving, and furniture you want to include.

Plot the space using the grids on page 184. (1 square equals 1 square foot of floor space). Plot your bath, including any adjacent closet, dressing room, hall, bedroom, and sitting or snacking areas that you'd like to remodel at the same time. One of the keys to making your bath beautiful and functional is good placement of doors, windows, fixtures, cabinetry, and built-in features such as shelving or towel warmers.

Use the architectural symbols below to mark the position of existing architectural features, if you're remodeling. Use a different color to indicate added features such as the placements of built-ins or new fixtures. Use dotted lines to mark obstructions, including prominent light fixtures and angled ceilings. If you're building a new addition, mark the existing structure in one color and use a different one to mark the addition.

Use the templates to experiment with different placements for fixtures, cabinetry, and built-in features. Trace or photocopy the appropriate items from the templates on the following pages and cut them out with a crafts knife or scissors. If you have furniture such as a reading chair or exercise equipment that you'd like to include in your new bath, measure and draw it to the same scale (1 square equals 1 square foot) on the grid paper.

Template Time

Use these templates to mark the placement of common bathroom components. The templates include both plan-view (top-down) and elevation (side view) perspectives, allowing you to create both floor plans and wall elevations. Most bath components are represented here, including various types and sizes of sinks, cabinets, showers, toilets, bidets, tubs, and more. Pay attention to details like door swings and drawer extensions (marked in dotted lines on these templates) as you consider the placement of these items in the room. If you don't see a template for something you'd like to include, draw your own.

Architectural Symbols

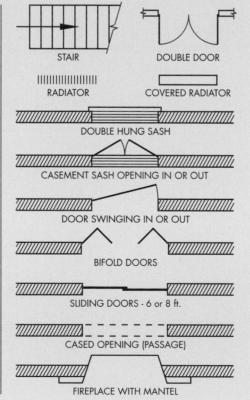

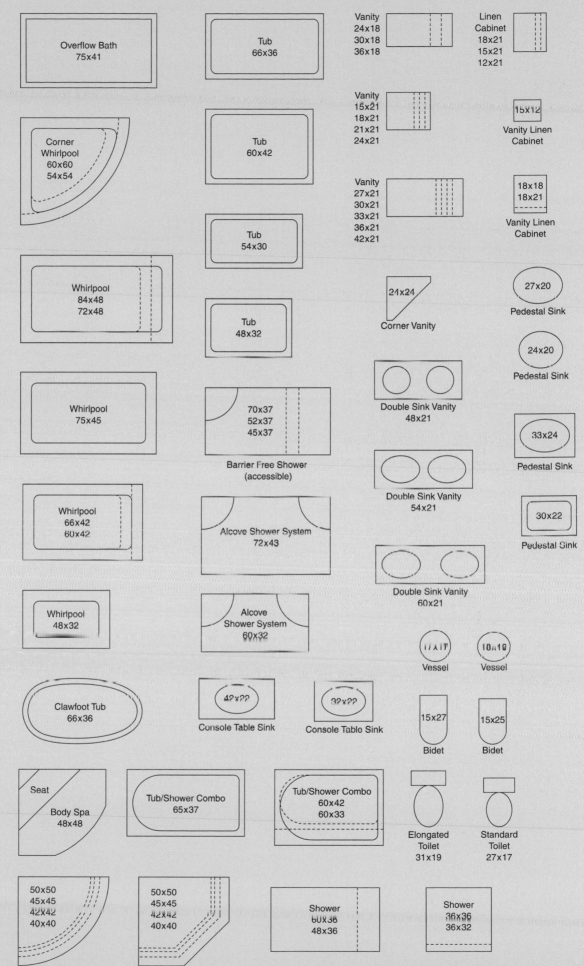

Overflow Bath
75x41

Tub
66x36

Vanity
24x18
30x18
36x18

Linen
Cabinet
18x21
15x21
12x21

Corner
Whirlpool
60x60
54x54

Tub
60x42

Vanity
15x21
18x21
21x21
24x21

Vanity Linen
Cabinet
15x12

Tub
54x30

Vanity
27x21
30x21
33x21
36x21
42x21

Vanity Linen
Cabinet
18x18
18x21

Whirlpool
84x48
72x48

Tub
48x32

Corner Vanity
24x24

Pedestal Sink
27x20

Whirlpool
75x45

Barrier Free Shower
(accessible)
70x37
52x37
45x37

Double Sink Vanity
48x21

Pedestal Sink
24x20

Pedestal Sink
33x24

Whirlpool
66x42
60x42

Alcove Shower System
72x43

Double Sink Vanity
54x21

Pedestal Sink
30x22

Whirlpool
48x32

Alcove
Shower System
60x32

Double Sink Vanity
60x21

Vessel
17x17

Vessel
10x10

Clawfoot Tub
66x36

Console Table Sink
42x22

Console Table Sink
32x22

Bidet
15x27

Bidet
15x25

Seat
Body Spa
48x48

Tub/Shower Combo
65x37

Tub/Shower Combo
60x42
60x33

Elongated
Toilet
31x19

Standard
Toilet
27x17

Corner Shower
50x50
45x45
42x42
40x40

Corner Shower
50x50
45x45
42x42
40x40

Shower
60x36
48x36

Shower
36x36
36x32

183

Planning Grid

Use a photocopier to reproduce the grid at its original size, then cut out the templates on page 182-183 to design your new or remodeled bathroom. 1 square = 1 square foot of floor space.

Bath Wish List

This checklist will help you identify what you'd like to have in your new bath. After each question or item, there's a place to rank its importance to you. Use the following number system, or devise your own: 1=must have, 2=want to have, 3=would be nice to have, but can do without.

Bath Evaluation

Whether you're building a brand-new bathroom or remodeling one, ask yourself the following questions to identify the things you really like in your current bath – or want to have – in the new one.

Traffic

____ Do doors block fixtures or storage when open?

____ Are paths from toilet to bathing to grooming areas logical?

____ Is/are the sink/s located closest to the most-used exit?

____ Is the bath equally accessible to all the bedrooms it services?

____ Are other traffic problems apparent?

Privacy

____ Are windows and treatments placed to allow both light and privacy?

____ Are toilet and bathing areas secluded from vanity areas?

____ Are latches and locks secure and easy for all users to operate?

Ventilation

Does the room have adequate natural ventilation via:

____ Skylights

____ Windows

____ Transom windows

____ French or sliding exterior doors

Is mechanical ventilation

____ Well-placed?

____ Effective?

____ Quiet?

Bathing

____ Are bathing facilities suitable for the intended use?

____ Is hot water supply adequate for the bathers' use?

____ Is water quality adequate, or does it require softening?

____ Are bathing areas adequately lit?

____ Are bathing areas easily accessible to all who will use them?

Are the following safety features present if needed:

____ Nonslip floors, tubs, shower stalls

____ Grip rails near toilets, tubs, and showers

____ Antiscald mixing valves on tubs and showers

Storage

____ Are bathing linens within reach of bathing facilities?

____ Is there a place for soiled laundry (chute, hamper, other)

____ Is there enough storage?

____ Could you relocate a passageway and reclaim space for cabinetry?

____ Would you like a walk-in closet?

____ A linen cabinet?

____ A cabinet for cleaning supplies?

Surfaces

____ Are you pleased with the current surfaces?

____ Are they easy to clean?

____ Do they tolerate standing water and high humidity well?

____ Do they resist staining, chipping, and scratching?

____ Is the flooring durable and attractive?

Light and views

____ Is your bath shadowy?

____ Do you have enough window light?

____ Do you have enough light for grooming or applying makeup?

____ Do window coverings and switches allow for varying amounts of light?

____ Can bathers enjoy views while retaining privacy?

OTHER

Would you like to include space in your bathroom for:

____ Exercising

____ Sitting

____ Reading the newspaper

____ Dressing

____ Enjoying a meal or snack

____ Making coffee

____ Watching television

____ Doing laundry

____ Ironing or folding clothes

____ Storing cleaning products

____ Storing linens

____ Displaying collections or decorative items

____ Other

Fixtures

____ Standard tub

____ Soaking tub

____ Whirlpool tub

____ Hot tub

____ Tub-and-shower combination

____ Shower stall

____ Double shower

____ Steam shower

____ Fixed showerhead

____ Handheld showerhead

____ Single vanity

____ Double vanity

____ Mirrors, vanity height

____ Mirrors, full-length

____ Toilet

____ Bidet

Luxury Features

____ Towel warmer

____ Radiant floor heating

____ Sauna

SMALL APPLIANCES

If you plan to use small appliances in your new or remodeled bath, fill out the following section so you can accommodate their space needs when you work up your design.

____ Toaster

____ Toaster oven

____ Cappuccino maker

____ Coffeemaker

____ Espresso maker

____ Mini fridge

____ Refrigerator drawers

Selecting a Pro

Choosing the best professionals to design and build your bathroom project makes your entire experience more enjoyable and ensures top-notch results. Whether you're searching for a designer, architect, or a contractor, use these tactics to track down the best one for you.

Gather. Collect the names of professionals to investigate and interview. Ask friends, relatives, and colleagues for suggestions and recommendations. Identify local referrals with the help of professional organizations such as the American Institute of Architects, 800/242-3837, www.aia.org; The National Kitchen and Bath Association, 877/NKBA-PRO, www.nkba.org; and The National Association of Home Builders Remodelers Council, 800/368-5242 Extension 8216, www.nahb.org.

Explore. Call the architects, designers, and remodeling contractors on your list—collect at least four to six from each profession you plan to use. Ask for references. Then contact the people they name and ask them to recount their positive and negative experiences. Also if you come across a recent remodeling project that you like, contact the homeowners and ask about their experiences and results.

Evaluate. Based on these references, interview the top three professionals in each profession who make the cut. Tour some of their finished projects. Savvy architects, designers, and contractors will ask you questions as well to determine your expectations and needs. You should come away from each interview and tour with a good idea of the quality of their work and how well their personalities and visions for the project match yours.

Solicit. To narrow your choice down to two or more architects or bathroom designers, it might be worth the additional cost to solicit preliminary drawings from each one. This is a great way to preview your working relationship. In the same vein, ask contractors for bids. Don't base your decision on cost alone. Weigh what you learned in the interview with the thoroughness of the bid itself.

Sign up. Before beginning a project with any professional, put the facts in writing to legally protect yourself before, during, and after the work is done. Define the scope of the project and fees as specifically as possible. The contract should include a clear description of the work to be done, materials that will be required, and who will supply the materials. It should spell out commencement and completion dates and any provisions relating to timeliness. A contract should also include your total costs (subject to additions and deductions by written change orders only). Tie the payments to work stages, and be wary of any contractor who wants a lot of money up front. If certain materials need to be ordered weeks in advance (to allow for manufacturing), get a list of those materials and their costs before committing to the idea of making a down payment. Baths usually require a sizable cash advance to finance appliances and cabinetry.

Stages and Phases

Prepare for your bath project by knowing what to expect during the process and ways of saving money. While no two remodeling projects are exactly the same, they generally follow this process:

Plan. During this stage you need to determine whether you'll use a design professional. Then finish the design and begin shaping the budget. When you are shopping for elements, find out how long it will take to receive the building and surface

1 *The workmanship evident in this vanity's granite countertop and cherry cabinetry wasn't left to chance. Check out your remodeling contractor thoroughly to make sure the quality of the installation is as good as the quality of the materials you specify.*

1 *High-quality amenities such as this jetted tub and marble surround cost money. Fortunately you have a variety of financing options, some of which may offer tax advantages, depending upon your situation.*

and air conditioning ductwork follow, then comes the insulation, drywall, roofing, and siding. Finish carpentry and electrical connections are next, followed by the flooring. Finally light fixtures and plumbing fixtures are installed.

Finish. Walk through the completed project with your contractor and architect, noting any concerns or unfinished details. The contractor follows up on your list in order to complete the project and receive final payment.

Remodeling Survival Tips

Even if someone else is doing the work, your bath (or an entire level or wing of your house if you're constructing a new master suite) becomes a construction zone, the mess can make you wonder if life will ever return to normal. To keep the inconveniences from becoming a major headache, discuss the project and your concerns with your contractor before the work begins.

At your preconstruction meeting (where you, the contractor, and the construction manager are present), ask for an overview of the entire process. Work together to develop a plan that minimizes disruption.

Discuss how the contractor will control dust. Most contractors tape a plastic barrier over doorways to reduce the amount of dust that escapes from the construction zone. Some also may tape off heat registers and change the furnace filters daily, especially when sanding drywall.

Request floor protection. Ask the contractor to cover all the

materials and fixtures once they are ordered. Be sure to build these time lags into the work schedule. Once the design is done, select a contractor, who may suggest alternative ways to accomplish some aspects of the design. During this phase you should finish the budget, select many of the products to be used, and determine a timeline for the project.

Confer. Invite the key players to your home: the architect or designer, contractor, primary subcontractors, as well as the job supervisor. Review all the particulars of the project and establish ground rules—including the daily start and finish times; how you'll keep the project site tidy—between you and the professionals you hire. Make sure you have a good communication plan: Put a notebook in a prominent location where both

you and the crew can jot down comments and questions.

Prepare. Remove your personal belongings from the job site. Prevent dust and debris from spreading throughout the house: Hang plastic sheeting and seal it securely between the job site and the rest of the house.

Demolish. Any built-in structures (cabinetry, counters, fixtures, or walls) that will not be included in the final project are removed during this stage. Doing the demolition yourself may save you money. If that's an option you'd like to explore, discuss it with your contractor during the plan and confer stages.

Construct. If you're building an addition, the foundation and framing go up first. Windows, plumbing, electrical wiring, heating, ventilation,

walkways and carpeted areas that lead to the construction zone with drop cloths or plastic runners.

Realize that noise is inevitable. Ask workers to arrive and leave at reasonable hours. Understand that if you set shorter workdays, you may lengthen the duration of the project.

Coordinate schedules. Tell the contractor in advance if there are any times, such as holidays or special family events, when your house will be off-limits to project work.

Funding Sources

You have a wide choice of ways to pay for your new bath.

With savings: If you've socked away enough money to fund your project, you're sitting pretty: There is no waiting, no finance costs, and no payments to make.

With income: By doing a major project in stages, you can put time on your side, paying for—and completing—portions of the work over set periods of time. This is another way to avoid finance costs. By stretching out the project, you'll have more time to shop for bargains on big-ticket items such as fixtures and cabinetry and to do some or all of the work yourself. However, working in stages prolongs the inconvenience of the project.

With a home equity loan: If you have enough equity in your home to pay for the bath you want, you may be able to finance the project with a lump-sum home equity loan. If you don't have enough savings to fund your project and you don't like the inconvenience of paying as you go, such a loan can be an attractive alternative. Interest on home equity loans is often tax-deductible and rates are generally lower than for consumer loans, making them an especially attractive option.

With a home equity line of credit: A home equity line of credit is even better than a home equity loan. Such a loan allows you to borrow up to a preset amount on a revolving credit account that works similarly to a credit card, but generally has lower rates and tax-deductible interest. The advantage over the lump-sum loan is that you only pay interest on money as you spend it. Since the cost of a remodeling is spread over time as you buy materials and pay contractors, the interest costs for a line of credit will be less than that of a lump-sum loan, all other factors being equal.

With a mortgage: If you're planning to remodel a home that you're about to buy, ask your lender about the possibility of getting a mortgage for the price of the home plus the price of the remodeling you desire. The interest will be tax-deductible, and the cost will spread out over the term of the loan, making this a relatively painless and money-savvy option.

With a credit card: This is generally the funding source of last resort because of high interest rates. However, this method can be useful if you're taking advantage of a low "teaser" interest rate, need to borrow a small amount, and/or if you can pay off your balance quickly. Be careful, because a combination of cost overruns, job delays, and "teaser" rate expiration dates can leave you with a big high-interest balance to pay.

With a combination of sources: Sometimes a patchwork of funding from a variety of sources is the way to go: You might have some savings, pay some as you go, pay for appliances with a retailer's promotion that offers no interest for a year, and contribute some of your own sweat equity to the project.

Controlling Costs

If your plans and projects are bigger than your billfold, use these tips to help you save dollars.

• **Choose materials wisely.** For example, birch cabinets cost two to three times less than solid cherry and can be finished with stains, paint, or stenciling. You also can buy stock cabinets and customize them with molding.

• **Get help.** Swap jobs with handy neighbors. Throw a theme party and feed guests. Ask family and friends to help out.

• **Assist as a general laborer.** If you're building an addition, consider doing simple grading, tearing up carpet, wallpapering, painting, and minor trim work and cleanup. A contract at cost-plus-fixed-fee credits your labor against a contractor's fee.

• **Be your own general contractor.** This is a full-time job, though, and not a task for the faint of heart. You need to understand the project the order of work to be done, and you must have a thorough knowledge of building codes.

• **Rent equipment** if you're completing part of the project yourself. Buying equipment often costs more.

• **Compare prices.** Your contractor gets a discount on many products, but you might pay less if you shop around and buy your own materials.

• **Keep the shape simple** if you're building an addition. A square foundation costs less than one with lots of angles. To add interest inside, angle interior walls, leave ceilings open to the roofline, and pay attention to finish details such as molding.

• **Plan around features that are costly to move,** such as plumbing stacks, heat runs, and chimneys. You'll reduce costs if you leave exterior openings—such as doors, windows, chimneys, plumbing stacks, kitchen vent fans, and the like—in their original locations.

Resources

A wealth of resources—from magazines to books to websites and interactive tools—can help give shape to your ideas. Get started with these resource suggestions.

Organizations

The National Kitchen and Bath Association
877/NKBA-PRO
www.nkba.org

Turn to this site for help finding a design professional in your area. You'll also find information on industry trends, products, and services. Request a free consumer workbook, browse designers' answers to common questions, and read articles on numerous aspects of bath design. Pictures of award-winning baths are posted as well.

The National Association of Home Builders
800/368-5242
www.nahb.org

This industry site also offers information for consumers who want to learn more about the home building and remodeling process. Everything from hiring professionals to insurance as well as surviving the process is covered. Information gets as specific as carpet care and how to maintain energy efficiency throughout a home.

Better Homes and Gardens Online Resources

Visit our website at www.bhg.com, where you'll find a wealth of ideas, inspiration, and help. Special features on the site include the following:

The BHG.com/Home Improvement Encyclopedia
Go to this site for help with interior and exterior improvement, repair projects and updates, information on do-it-yourself projects, calculators to help estimate costs and materials, and a tool dictionary.

Home Solutions
Turn here for everything from quick fixes to remodeling project ideas.

Decorating Center
From design lessons to projects and ideas, you'll find inspiration and help here.

Painting Center
Click on this site to find painting projects, ideas and help with interior, exterior, and decorative painting techniques and color choices.

Arrange-A-Room
This interactive tool lets you lay out any room in your house without straining your back.

Ready, Set, Organize
Find efficient, inspired storage ideas and get help with clutter control.

Magazines

Better Homes and Gardens magazine and its Special Interest Publications.

   Kitchen & Bath Ideas
   Kitchen Planning Guide
   Kitchen & Bath Products Guide
   Remodeling Ideas
   Remodeling Products Guide

Also:
Country Home magazine
Traditional Home magazine
Decorator Showcase magazine
Renovation Style magazine

Books
Kitchen Planner
Bath Planner
Deck Planner
Exterior Style Planner
Complete Decks
Complete Kitchens
Complete Basements, Attics, and Bonus Rooms

Building Codes

Building codes are designed to protect the structural integrity of your home, safeguarding your health and safety and that of your family, friends, and anyone who comes in contact with your home. Before you plan a remodeling project, visit your location's building department. Doing so will help you take your ideas farther and may well be one of the most enlightening 15 minutes that you invest in your project. Be prepared to tell the officials what you're thinking of doing—even if your ideas are rough—and ask them what building codes will apply. A rough sketch of the available space and location of windows, doors, and mechanical systems will make your visit even more productive. Don't be dissuaded if local codes call for a standard you can't meet. Ask about exceptions; many officials are willing to make them to accommodate existing buildings if safety or practicality isn't compromised.

The building department of your town or city government will likely be your governing building official and source of building codes. If you live outside city limits, the clerk or commissioner may perform this function at the county level. Occasionally county officials will not govern a property and you'll need to call the state departments of building standards or housing to find a governing official.

Index

Better Homes and Gardens

dream the perfect home,
then make it a reality.

Look for these great **Home Improvement** titles—wherever books are sold.